Great Buildings of the World

MODERN BUILDINGS

by John Winter

PAUL HAMLYN

LONDON · NEW YORK · SYDNEY · TORONTO

Published by the Hamlyn Publishing Group Limited,
Hamlyn House, The Centre, Feltham, Middlesex

© THE HAMLYN PUBLISHING GROUP LIMITED 1969

Printed and bound in Great Britain by
Morrison and Gibb Limited, London and Edinburgh

Endpapers :   *Palace of Labour, Turin*   (*Le Corbusier*)

Frontispiece :   *Office and Research Building, Dorman Long
Steel Works, Middlesbrough* (*model*)

Contents

8

INTRODUCTION

When we look at the world around us, it is sometimes difficult to believe that our age has produced any great buildings at all. Medieval towns may have been squalid, Elizabethan architecture may have been brash, Victorian buildings may seem neurotic, but it is during the 20th century that the face of the earth has been despoiled on the grand scale. Meaningless towns spring up and featureless suburbs spread mile after dreary mile across the land. Fine old cities like Worcester in England or Boston in Massachusetts lose their individual centres to faceless new developments, presumably in order to make money for somebody. Mediocrity prevails and one might assume that the art of architecture is dead, killed by apathy, ignorance, regulations and committees, and that only the old quarters of cities have any character and honesty.

Yet, for those who take the trouble to look, there is much hope; for paradoxically we have created, alongside the mess, some of the greatest works of architecture ever built. They are not very numerous, and have to be searched out, for society today is not an architecture-oriented society in the way it was six hundred years ago, when the most prominent buildings would be designed by the most talented men of the time and the wealth of the community devoted to their realisation. Twentieth-century society is confused, and its chaos is revealed in our dismal new buildings, while only the strongest architects working with single-minded clients have been able to act with any clarity. Never has the gap between the best and the ordinary been so great, and this in spite of the mass dissemination of ideas and the most numerous and highly trained architectural profession that has ever existed.

In any age, the most important buildings have always reflected the

Mies van der Rohe's 1920 project of a glass skyscraper could not have been realised at that time, but it demonstrates the objectives architects were striving for at the period. Its siting among the buildings of an historic German town illustrates the desire to shock conventional taste present in any revolutionary movement.

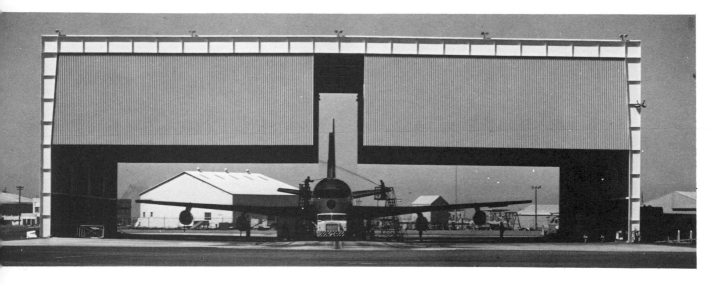

dominant preoccupations of the civilisations that produced them: the ancient Egyptians' concern with death, the Roman will to power, the religious fervour of the middle ages, the Renaissance concern with classical learning and the overbearing confidence of Victorian England. Today we live in an age dominated by technology, so it follows that only buildings that reflect this facet of contemporary life are included in this book.

To illustrate the operation of technology, let us take a man travelling by air. Consider the aircraft in which he flies, one of the most beautiful products of our time; consider too the sophistication of its controls. The plane lands and the man drives away in his car. Consider his car, how it is made and the satisfaction he gets from driving it. At the end of his journey he arrives at his house; now consider the house, the way it is made and its comfort or lack of it. How is it possible that the civilisation that produced the plane and the car also produced the house? Is it not extraordinary that we, who have evolved such splendid machines, should still build houses in the same old primitive way? Further, is it not obvious that as long as we continue to do so we shall always be acutely short of houses, so that millions are forced to live in slums and thousands on the streets?

It is difficult to say precisely why building should lag so far behind other fields of production. Among the delaying factors are the sentimentality and conservatism of some owners, planning authorities and building societies, which often hold back develop-

Unlike the glass skyscraper project, where the architect romanticised a technology that was not yet available, Skidmore, Owings and Merrill's Wash hangar at San Francisco Airport (above), designed by pupils of Mies van der Rohe, shows an easy familiarity with the sophisticated technology of thirty-five years later. The production was a straightforward, unromanticised, but very beautiful structure for a routine mechanical operation.

The living room of the house, right, overlooking Long Island Sound, designed by Philip Johnson in 1955, epitomises the possibilities opened up by new technology. For thousands of years people had lived in solid, ground-hugging dwellings; now a dramatic site can be exploited by a glassy room, elegantly poised above it.

ment in house building and enforce very low standards. Building regulations are written with a traditional, hand-made house in mind, so the innovator is always working with his hands tied behind his back. Further, many of the machine-made, logically designed houses that have been built have been more crude and unattractive than the hand-made products they set out to supersede. But ultimately the situation is not open to choice. The demand for houses is too great for a craft-oriented industry; thus only the architects who are exploring in the realm of machine-made buildings can have any real relevance for the future. This is not speculation but a question of fact; the buildings of the next generation may be better or worse than those of the past, but they will certainly be different, to keep pace with new technology and new requirements. It is for the architect of the future to meet the challenge of these demands and techniques and to make magical places in machine-made structures. The buildings selected for this book exemplify situations where the

New building methods demand a constant reappraisal of any aesthetic dogma. The Alcoa building, above, in San Francisco is ruggedly braced against wind and earthquake.

Right, day and night views of the weekend house designed by Philip Johnson for his own use. Efficient artificial light is beginning to be used as a major element in architecture. Here, for example, guests can dine with only the floodlit trees for illumination.

12

facts of the modern world have been accepted and some measure of poetry has emerged.

In order to produce truly meaningful buildings, architects, throughout history, have shared in and identified themselves with the ideas and ideals of the society in which they live, whether it is the glorification of God, pope or monarch, or the democratic and materialistic bent of our own time. Of course many of today's architects treat their profession as just a job they do to earn a living; they may build most of the buildings but it is the minority who really care that design the buildings that matter, and members of this minority group will usually have strong feelings about the modern world.

A factor that has a strong influence on modern architects dedicated to the design of meaningful buildings is the gap, both physical and artistic, between how people live and how they could live. The housing shortage is a recurrent sore on the conscience of architects today and a constant spur to the quest for newer, better and more economical building techniques. Buckminster Fuller has said that the achievement of the good life for one man depends on the realisation of the good life for every man, and it is the search for general rather than specific solutions that is modern architecture's chief concern. This is why great modern buildings, as exemplified by the selection in this book, consist not of whimsical or highly personal buildings but of typical structures in which any of us might live,

The distribution of essential service runs is a major building problem. The Richards Laboratories building at the University of Pennsylvania (1960–5), left, is the most famous attempt made so far to use service runs as a major means of architectural expression and earned it the nickname ducthenge.

Below, the Bauhaus building at Dessau, built in 1926 and the first major modern building. Designed by Walter Gropius, its director, it was the only school at which modern design was systematically taught until the late 1930s.

Above, the villa at Poissy designed by Le Corbusier at the end of the 1920s. It is a poetic statement in reinforced concrete—the first 20th-century building to match in quality the great buildings of history.

Richard Neutra, a Viennese who had worked with the leading European modern architects, emigrated to America in 1923. Opposite, his Lovell House, built in Los Angeles in 1928, which took the European modern movement across the Atlantic, although America remained conservative architecturally until after the Second World War.

Left, the house at Wentworth, Surrey, by the young architects Connell, Ward and Lucas, exemplifying the productive period in England— the late 1930s, when about fifty modern houses were built that were unsurpassed elsewhere.

work or learn: they are offices, houses, factories, not cathedrals.

In the past, important buildings proclaimed their grandeur by rich carving and decoration. In a civilisation where everything is made by hand, the ornamentation of buildings was a time-consuming and expensive operation, and thus conferred status upon the building and its owner. With the coming of the Industrial Revolution in the 19th century, machines were made to produce ornament, which was stamped out by the mile, often in the crudest possible way; cheap buildings could be covered with ornament and often were. Thus the whole traditional value of ornament disintegrated and modern architects, in reaction, have found the form of construction satisfying enough without adornment and welcomed the simple products that machines could make.

In earlier societies the pace of change was slow, and buildings, constructed with solid walls of stone or brick, were regarded as permanent. The architect could therefore satisfactorily tailor his building to its function. Modern society, on the other hand, changes fast and the rate of change accelerates continually. The demands placed upon a building may shift equally fast, and a building that is fitted to its initial function too closely may soon be outmoded. Already most buildings in our city centres are used for purposes entirely different to those for which they were built, usually with considerable loss of efficiency and convenience. With modern methods of construction—taking the load of a building on the frame rather than on solid walls—it is possible to design buildings that can be endlessly changed, but even this technique may not be flexible enough. One of the images constantly recurring in the work of the youngest generation of architects is the building so fluid that it is never completed but is permanently surmounted by cranes, which continually rebuild it to ever fresh requirements.

If the magic has gone from ornament, and the form of a building is no longer directly related to its function, what have we left with which to create an architecture? One answer is the means of construction, and it is in the erection of elegant structures that modern architects have excelled. The proportions of its structure, the quality of the detailing of its joints and junctions—the way glass is joined to wood, or steel is joined to plastic—are points at which the endless toil of the good architect shows, and it is here that we will find the architecture of our own time. And just as a knowledge of the five orders is an advantage in appreciating classical buildings, so a knowledge of modern construction, together with an acquaintance

The Kaufmann house, built at Bear Run, Pennsylvania in 1936, is the closest Frank Lloyd Wright ever came to the European modern movement. His career, spanning seventy years, was one of high adventure and great creativity.

Postwar England was a time of limited resources and social idealism and pre-fabricated schools, such as the one at Hitchin, left, exemplifying the best work of the time.

with the history of the modern movement in architecture, is helpful in understanding the work of the best contemporary architects.

Put a man in a beautiful stretch of countryside; for a while he is happy and enjoys the view, but then rain, snow or wind spoils his pleasure. So we put a roof over him, and four glass walls around him so that he can still enjoy the view and for a while he is happy again and admires the landscape. Soon, however, he complains that it is too cold or too stuffy or too dark, and so we have to give him heating and ventilation and lighting and we are at once involved in the whole new world of building services. Services have made possible the permanent habitation of the desert and the poles and the temporary habitation of outer space and regions under the sea. They have made life in buildings comfortable and, incidentally, have revealed new delights in our cities—nothing is so excitingly urban as Manhattan at night—and new pleasures in the countryside. Snowy landscape is most pleasant when the viewer is behind double glazing with his central heating.

In a modern structure, such as an air-conditioned office building, services may occupy as much as 30 per cent of the volume of the

Postwar Europe was poor, but America was rich, and its citizens patronised their architects lavishly, as in Richard Neutra's Tremaine house, right, built in Santa Barbara in 1947.

building and take 50 per cent of the budget. Many modern architects look back wistfully to the past and envy their predecessors who worked in the days before plumbing. 'For Ledoux, it was easy; no pipes', said Le Corbusier of an early 19th-century architect. But plumbing is here to stay, and the mass of wires, pipes and ducts that have to be threaded through buildings grow larger every year. The effect of services on architectural form has been surprisingly little discussed, although in 1957 the American architect Louis Kahn started a furore in architectural circles by designing a laboratory building in which the towers containing the services stood as the major architectural statement of a building that was too serious for architects to ignore—and earned it the nickname 'ducthenge'. Other architects have designed office buildings with air-conditioning ducts or lift towers on the outside. But generally the architectural expression of service elements has been small, because it is usually most convenient to group them in the middle of a building, where they are easy to insulate and maintain, and to keep the outside for rooms that need windows.

Yet while the direct impact of service runs on architecture may have been small, the difference made by these services has been enormous. It is hard to imagine that only a hundred years ago

buildings were murky places after nightfall and many people went
to bed at sundown because their houses were so dark and dismal.
Now lighting is a normal part of all buildings and a dramatic part of
some. For example, the American architect Philip Johnson found
that the glass-walled country house he designed for himself in 1949
looked black and dull from the inside after dark. So he installed
clusters of floodlights to illuminate the surrounding trees and now,
at night, the house seems an oasis in a fantastic landscape, surrounded
by real trees as decoration. This is obviously an extreme example,
but everywhere lighting is becoming an important element in architectural design, and the photographs in current architectural periodicals include many night shots.

The combination of electric light and artificial ventilation means
that rooms, which formerly had always been placed on the outside
walls of buildings, can now be placed anywhere and buildings of
great bulk can and are being built. The Krupp office building at
Rheinhausen, for example, is 150 feet by 200 feet and, since natural
light is effective only 15 or 20 feet from a window, most of its inhabitants rely on artificial light as well as artificial ventilation. In other
words, windows have ceased to be a practical necessity, and certain
kinds of buildings such as bowling alleys and cinemas are built
without them. In the United States, windowless office blocks and
windowless schools have been built, but this hardly seems sensible,
for windows, deprived of their old function of admitting light and
air, take on a new role as a psychological necessity.

The modern movement in architecture is now old enough to have
a history of its own, and since obviously none of the buildings in this
book was designed in isolation, some knowledge of this history is
necessary to understand why they are as they are. For modern
buildings, like any other, are part of a historical movement; it is
therefore helpful to outline the main trends in architecture during
the last 120 years or so.

During the 19th century building was characterised by a split
between the professions: the architects, who covered their buildings
with decorations copied from the buildings of the past to give them
status, and the engineers, practical men, unhampered by aesthetic
ideas, who used the new technology of iron to give us the Crystal
Palace, Brooklyn Bridge, King's Cross station and the Eiffel Tower.
24 In retrospect, it is the engineers who are seen to have created the

The year 1952 saw the completion of Le Corbusier's Unité d'Habitation in Marseille (above)
and Skidmore, Owings and Merrill's Lever
House in Park Avenue, New York (right). The
simultaneous completion of these two buildings
revealed that modern architecture was no longer
the cohesive movement it had been ten years
before. Marseille was technically crude, aesthetically stunning; Lever was technically
superb, but perhaps a little glib.

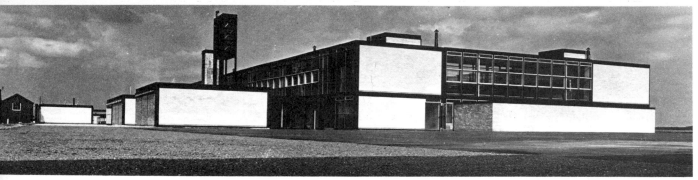

real masterpieces of the period, and it is from their work that our own architecture is in part descended.

In one city only did men of the calibre of the Victorian engineers become involved in large-scale building. This was in Chicago, which must have been very much 'in the provinces' in terms of Victorian culture. In 1871 the centre of Chicago was razed by fire; this was followed by a real-estate boom in the business district, where large sums were to be made by speculative building. The salesmen from Hiram Otis's firm came and offered architects the mechanical elevator and the skyscraper was invented to reap the most profit from crowded sites; but the brick walls of high buildings grew so thick that the point of diminishing returns was soon reached. The salesmen from Carnegie then came with their newly developed

Above, two views of the school at Hunstanton, Norfolk, completed in 1954 to the designs of Alison and Peter Smithson, then still in their twenties. The first postwar British building to be powerful architecturally, it marks the emergence of the new generation.

Bessemer steel and offered architects the steel frame for building. Thus architecture's most profound revolution was carried out without fuss. Now, instead of buildings with massive walls, structures of unprecedented height could be supported on comparatively few steel posts. Also the glass industry responded with plate glass, which could fill the spaces between the columns, and the pneumatic caisson (which, like the steel frame, was pioneered by the bridge builders) was introduced to support the steel columns on the Chicago mud. Building was no longer in the charge of the rule-of-thumb traditionalists; the new methods demanded skilled technicians to undertake the design and erection of buildings. During the forty years that followed the fire, the loop area of Chicago was rebuilt with splendid buildings, many of which still stand as a challenge for us to do better.

The first of the pioneer modern architects was Frank Lloyd Wright, who worked in Chicago during its most creative period. But later he

A row of houses in Chicago designed by Y. C. Wong exemplifies the cool, sophisticated, straightforwardness of the work of Mies van der Rohe's students.

reacted against cities and concentrated on the problem of the suburban house and by 1910 he had built many of his 'Prairie Houses', low-spreading and with open plans, which were eagerly studied by the young architects in Europe.

In Europe generally, the years immediately preceding the first World War saw the collapse of Art Nouveau and the laying of much of the ground work and the working out of much of the theoretical basis for modern architecture. Few important buildings were built, but the pioneers of the modern movement—Walter Gropius, Le Corbusier, Mies van der Rohe—built their first, rather tentative buildings during this period.

The war was followed by the 'heroic' period in continental Europe—a time when the issues were clear, emotions strong and compromises non-existent. In Germany, Gropius developed the Bauhaus, a school of art, architecture and allied subjects, committed to modern design. He also designed its building at Dessau, the first major masterpiece of modern architecture in Europe.

In 1927 Mies van der Rohe organised a housing exhibition at Stuttgart and invited all the leading European moderns to design houses. The result was a little suburb of white-walled, flat-roofed dwellings, for during this 'heroic' period the moderns were more or less agreed on questions of style. Meanwhile in France, Le Corbusier built a series of houses, culminating in the marvellous luxury dwellings at Garches and Poissy. In America Richard Neutra, trained under the European moderns and Frank Lloyd Wright, built houses in Los Angeles. Antonin Raymond built similar houses in

The administrative offices of United Air Lines at Des Plaines, Illinois. Designed by Skidmore, Owings and Merrill, it shows the preoccupation with the structural frame common to those trained by Mies.

Japan and the phrase 'the international style' was applied to modern architecture.

In the 1930s Nazism in Germany and depression in Western Europe brought the great continental movement to a halt. In France, Le Corbusier built only a few small houses, and in Germany the moderns literally ran for their lives. At this point England came into her own, and for a few brief years in the late 1930s the moderns based on London were the most significant group of architects anywhere; the Highpoint block (described in this book) represents their work at its best. Refugees from the continent brought skill and status to the English movement, which it lost when threat of war made many of them travel on to the United States.

During the war years, only neutral countries like Sweden, Switzerland and Brazil continued to build and to develop their architecture. Architects from the combattant nations, demobbed and in practice again, found the architectural periodicals full of buildings from these countries, which therefore had a great influence at this time. In England, extreme shortage of school buildings led to interesting new techniques of school construction, but this field of development rapidly lost architectural impetus and became technocratic and rather dull. In the United States, Neutra, Gropius and Mies van der

This house near Los Angeles by Craig Ellwood shows the influence of Mies van der Rohe's crisp steel-framed buildings on the design of a one-family house.

Above, an example of a plastic dome by Buckminster Fuller, who brought the technology of the space industry into building.

Opposite, top, the vast complex of the Air Force Academy at Colorado Springs by Skidmore, Owings and Merrill. By the mid-1950s, the influence of Miesian architecture was so strong in the United States that even the government became a patron.

Opposite, bottom, buildings for a summer camp, designed by Ed Barnes of New York, showing a relaxed approach to design only possible when the heroic phase of modern architecture was over, and a new generation of architects accepted modern as the norm.

As Europe moved out of the phase of acute postwar shortage, so the influence of Le Corbusier's rugged building declined and some buildings were constructed with technical sophistication, as was the Danish house, left, by Arne Jacobsen. 31

Rohe were established as teachers, and it is their pupils who dominate the American scene from 1950 onwards.

In the late 1940s the main pioneers of the 'heroic' period took on a new lease of life, and by the early 1950s the rather pedestrian architecture of Sweden and Switzerland lost its pre-eminence to the work of this second creative period of the Masters. Neutra's Tremaine house, Le Corbusier's Marseille building, Mies's 860 Lakeshore Drive were eye-openers for postwar architects. But these three men, whose buildings had looked so similar in 1927, were now following

Less way-out than Buckminster Fuller and more in tune with the requirements of the building industry as it exists is Jean Prouvé, a French pressed-metal designer. This Air France holiday centre south of Paris, with its pressed-metal columns, wall panels and roof typifies his work.

The Engineering Laboratories at Leicester University, designed by Stirling and Gowan and completed in 1964, emphasise the various parts of the building—lecture halls, laboratories, staircase and so on are each expressed as separate entities.

Left, the Economist building in St James's Street, London, designed by Alison and Peter Smithson and completed in 1964. Cool modern buildings, informally grouped, form a piazza within the site.

Right, a model of the new headquarters building for Boots near Nottingham, completed 1968, designed by Skidmore, Owings and Merrill of Chicago. As in other fields, American know-how spreads around the world and here is manifestly superior to the local products.

Below right, a helicopter placing the air-conditioning equipment into a new, system-built Californian school. Such developments take building away from the crafts tradition to become an industrial product.

This introduction started with a glass tower designed by Mies van der Rohe and ends with his apartment building (far right) completed in 1966 in Baltimore. All the buildings in this book were built within a professional lifetime, but during that period the young revolutionaries became the established masters.

widely divergent paths and the coherent movement was no more. Just as a psychologist may follow the teachings of Jung or Freud or someone else, so there are different schools in recent modern architecture. Halen (Chapter 9) and Roehampton (Chapter 10) are Corbusian while Hunstanton and the Rosen House are Miesian. The Miesians in America achieved a dominant position in the mid-1950s and built major buildings for the Establishment, such as the Air Force Academy at Colorado Springs. However, slick derivatives of the Miesian glass tower led to a general reaction against this type of architecture at the end of the decade.

During all this time Buckminster Fuller was building his domes and other technocrats, notably Jean Prouvé in France, were experimenting with sophisticated building techniques.

It is risky to generalise about the present, but while the objective approach in America is continued by Mies and his students with such works as the California Schools Systems Development, it seems that architecture in general (particularly on the East Coast) has a more wilful quality and that its influence has declined. In Germany the influence of Mies van der Rohe, with his Germanic love of perfection, continues unchallenged, and there are many successful Miesian practices.

In England the completion of the Leicester laboratories by Stirling and Gowan and the Economist Building by the Smithsons announced the arrival of a new generation determined to equal the quality of the best English work of the 1930s, and the welcome employment of the best foreign architects—Arne Jacobsen from Denmark for St Catherine's College, Oxford; Ralph Erskine, a British architect practising in Sweden, for Clare Hall, Cambridge; Skidmore, Owings and Merrill of New York for the Heinz Building at Hillingdon; SOM of Chicago for the new Boots Headquarters at Nottingham; and the commissioning, in his 82nd year, of Mies van der Rohe for an office building in the city of London. English architecture, so provincial in the 1940s and 1950s, has become international again.

Inevitably the selection of any 12 buildings without the perspective given by time is an arbitrary exercise and one that is influenced by personal taste. Architects like Y. C. Wong, designer of the modest court houses in Chicago, might be surprised to find their buildings labelled 'great'; other buildings described in this book, such as Seagram and Marseille, are established masterpieces. History, looking back on our period, may choose a different 12. We shall have to wait and see.

CHAPTER 1

UNITÉ D'HABITATION

Boulevard Michelet, Marseille

The American architect Eero Saarinen has described Le Corbusier as the Leonardo da Vinci of our time, a prolific writer, poet, painter and architect whose ideas and theories have profoundly influenced the work of three generations of architects. His buildings are among the most powerful works of architecture that have ever been built. Yet they are not just magnificent buildings but are also expressions of Le Corbusier's theories of the good life and the good city. Indeed, he designed a great city before he built anything of significance and all his buildings are seen by him as prototype parts for the city. As an urban man, he reacted against the suburban ideal of a house in its own garden, although during his first decade of practice (in the 1920s) his only commissions were for suburban houses, which he accepted joyfully and designed beautifully; even so, each one was seen by him as a prototype unit for a large block of flats.

The prewar buildings of Le Corbusier were precisely made and carefully put together, and when he reopened his office in 1945, architects looked to him to give them a lead with even more polished buildings. The war was scarcely over when Le Corbusier was invited by the Ministry of Reconstruction to design the Unité d'Habitation at Marseille, a building to house 1500 people. Typically, he accepted the commission on condition that he could ignore all building controls and regulations! As design work proceeded, Le Corbusier found that machine-made materials, which had been the very basis of the new architecture, were hard to come by or costly in postwar France; even the steel frame proved too expensive. To be given the commission he had been waiting for all his life, and then to be denied the materials to build it, would have driven a lesser man to despair. But Le Corbusier displayed an inventiveness that left his admirers gasping. Single handed and as the result of one building, he changed the course of European architecture by making crude concrete a material of great emotional impact.

Concrete had always been a favourite material in modern architecture and the early houses of Le Corbusier were no exception. But the concrete had always been plastered over and painted to give it a smooth, clean-cut finish. For it was part of the credo of early modern architecture that building parts should be made by machine —an attitude so deep-rooted that even buildings laboriously made by hand were precisely finished to give them a machine-made look. In the Marseille building, Le Corbusier abandoned the difficult search for a smoothly finished, accurately made concrete and instead revealed and celebrated the technique of making it. Concrete is poured in place into wooden moulds and allowed to set. The mould is then removed but its precise form stays permanently imprinted on to the concrete. Le Corbusier's moulds were made up of rough boards, placed a fraction of an inch apart and arranged in patterns so that the concrete emerged as a rugged, masculine material of great personality, which could be made with reasonable economy in France in the late 1940s and handled by workmen without a high degree of skill. (If a board was a quarter of an inch or so out of

The Unité as seen from the Boulevard Michelet, right, reveals its function: an area of small windows rising up left of centre marks the staircase and lift positions; to the right of this, and halfway up the building, is the shopping centre— a double floor treated very differently. At the extreme left the wall is blank, for the end flats are turned to catch the southern sun. At ground level, the land flows through and the block is held aloft on massive concrete columns.

Left, the site plan. Note how the building is placed obliquely, so that it seems to fit the oddly-shaped site; this also enables the living rooms to face either due east or due west, which Le Corbusier considered the optimum aspect for a building in this latitude.

Right, a section cut through three typical floors in the building showing the rue intérieure *in the centre giving access to all the dwellings on three floors. The upper maisonette (shaded grey) has its double-height living room to the right; the lower dwelling has its double-height living room to the left and is entered at the level of the gallery in that room.*

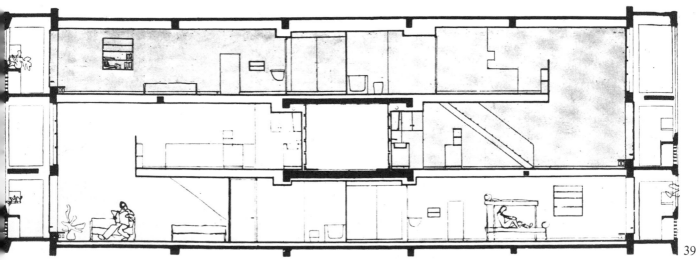

position it did not matter.) The building took five years to complete and during that time streams of architects from all over the world came to visit the site—so many that they interfered with the progress of the work and barbed-wire fences were erected to keep them out! They came to experience for themselves the power of the raw concrete—*béton brut* as Le Corbusier called it—and to decide for themselves whether this new rugged, crumbly architecture was indeed that of the future. At first, architects were shocked and accused Le Corbusier of abandoning modern architecture for peasant and romantic forms; but Le Corbusier himself seemed to revel in the poor workmanship and on the day the building was opened he said: 'How often visitors (particularly the Swiss, the Dutch and the Swedes) have said to me, "Your building is beautiful, but how badly it has been executed". But I reply, "Have you never noticed in the cathedrals and the châteaux how the stones are roughly shaped, the faults being admitted or even cleverly exploited? Perhaps you do not notice these things when you are looking at architecture; but in men and women do you not see the wrinkles and the birthmarks, the crooked noses, the innumerable peculiarities? Have you come expecting to meet the Venus de Medici in flesh and blood?"'

Above, an example of the way in which Le Corbusier, faced with the lack of skill and machinery in Europe in 1946, deliberately emphasised and enjoyed the crudeness of concrete poured into rough timber moulds.

In all Le Corbusier's postwar buildings, every dimension is made to conform to the modulor, *a series of measurements related to one another and to the human body. An explanation of the system is cast in concrete by the entrance of the Marseille Unité, above left.*

The Unité, opposite, is built to house 1600 people, their shopping, recreation and sports facilities in a single building. It is an extreme reaction to the garden-city idea, which Le Corbusier considered overemphasised the family at the expense of communal living.

41

The point was made, and during the decade that followed, architects in Europe, Japan and the United States were deliberately making their concrete rough in an attempt to obtain some of the powerful character of the Marseille building. In retrospect however it would seem that the magic of Marseille comes from the genius of Le Corbusier himself, who alone can imbue rough concrete with such passion. In subsequent buildings in France and India, Le Corbusier has again made masterpieces out of raw, unfinished concrete, but wherever the idea has been copied by other architects the magic has evaporated and only the bad workmanship remains. Le Corbusier and Mies van der Rohe are the two great architects of modern times, but while some of the generation influenced by the logic of Mies have built very successful Miesian buildings, Le Corbusier's incredible ability to create marvellous forms is his own personal gift, and is therefore less easy for other architects to imitate.

Le Corbusier believes that land is very precious and that a traditional building wastes the land it stands on. His buildings, he claims, gain extra land, for they are raised off the ground on stilts and the roof is used as a terrace or playground. At Marseille, the building is raised high off the ground on elephantine columns so that children can play and cars can drive underneath. (It may seem to be stretching a point to run to the expense of raising the whole building for the sake of such marginal advantages, but to Le Corbusier it was a principle of his architectural philosophy. Just as in the 1930s Le Corbusier saw his houses as prototypes for the apartment buildings he would like to build, so, after the war, Le Corbusier saw Marseille as a fragment of a replanned city, in which it was essential for the ground to flow under the buildings.) Having freed the ground under the building, Le Corbusier set about using the roof space; here, as if on the deck of a great liner high above the city with the sea on one side and the Alpes Maritimes on the other he has placed a crèche, a pool, a gymnasium and one of the most astonishing collections of shapes ever created. This is a garden of fantastic sculpture, 450 feet long and 80 feet wide, with steps, pools, fountains, ramps and viewing platforms, all made with raw concrete into a never-never land for grown-ups. It is architecture run riot, yet controlled as only a genius can. No other architect can imitate this, nor have they risked the attempt; they can only marvel at the power of invention of its creator.

Le Corbusier saw himself not just as an architect, but also as a social reformer, with a vision of a coherent, orderly city of great

42

Above, the two-storey-high living room of the lower dwelling in the section on page 39; the kitchen-eating area is on the gallery.

buildings, open spaces and trees. The Marseille building is not just a block of flats but, as Le Corbusier would call it, a 'vertical garden city', with its own shopping street half-way up the building, its own hotel, school, barber's shop, café and all the requirements of day-to-day living. Not all the amenities have proved a success in practice but then no building has ever before introduced so many new ideas all at once. The idea of catering for so many everyday requirements within one building has been little imitated. This is partly because the financing of large apartment buildings is such that non-residential uses are not encouraged, but mainly because people are becoming increasingly mobile and so can seek out other shops in preference to those provided on their doorstep. But if the shopping floor at Marseille has no progeny, the layout of the flats themselves has begotten offspring around the world—for example, at Roehampton in England and at Halen in Switzerland.

Left, a view of a typical living room, two storeys high with a gallery inside and a balcony outside. 43

Le Corbusier allocated his time very strictly, and for much of his life worked as a painter during the morning and as an architect in the afternoon. (On air trips, when he could neither paint nor draw, he wrote poems!) As an architect, he always admired the spaces in the studios of his painter friends (such spaces are usually the height of two normal rooms and have a gallery at one side) and consciously used this concept to give to a small dwelling the sense of grandeur and spaciousness that only height can give. So at Marseille the living rooms are all two-storeys high, with the outside wall fully glazed, opening on to a balcony the full width of the room. In each living room is a gallery, which contains either a dining kitchen or the parents' bedroom. This arrangement is admirably suited to families with small children, but it must cause domestic chaos when the children become teenagers and, say, play records with their friends in the living room while their parents are trying to sleep on a gallery in the same room! From this big double-height space containing kitchen, living, dining and parents' sleeping areas, there is a long tail extending through the building; this tail contains the bathroom and other service rooms and two long thin bedrooms for children, which extend to the other side of the block and have their own balcony. Each apartment, with a two-storey living room on one side and a single-storey tail on the other, is interlocked with another apartment facing the other way. Thus there are two apartments in every three storeys of height, in the middle of which is the access corridor. This access *rue intérieure*, as Le Corbusier called it, is in the centre of the building and has no windows; it is rather dark and the wonderful views from the building are kept as a surprise for the visitor until he is inside an apartment.

In any high-density housing development, it is essential to make buildings as thick as possible if the apparent bulk is to be played down. For example, a 25 per cent increase in the thickness of a block may be hardly noticeable but a 25 per cent increase in height may change the surrounding areas out of all recognition. At Marseille, Le Corbusier has packed his accommodation in by making a very deep building—80 feet from one face to the other. This means that access corridors and minor rooms such as bathrooms are deep inside the building with artificial light and ventilation while the children's bedrooms are very long and thin. But these inconveniences may well be a small price to pay for incorporating all the accommodation in a single block, so that views on each side are of greenery, mountains and sea and not of a building a few hundred feet away.

44

Two views of the roof, one of architecture's magic places and a playground for young and old. Commanding views of the blue Mediterranean and the Alpes Maritimes, it has a nursery school, a gymnasium, a running track, a bar, an open-air theatre and many places for just sitting and enjoying the space.

Le Corbusier has compared the construction of the flats to bottles in a bottle rack. First a framework of concrete—the bottle rack—is built and into it are fitted the flats—the bottles—each an independent structure resting on the frame on pads of lead to reduce the transmission of noise from flat to flat. Construction elements that are repeated a great number of times—such as balcony fronts—are precast since this is economic where a large number of identical units are required. Precast concrete is poured into a mould on the site or in a factory and transported to its position as a solid mass and bolted in. Its size is therefore limited by the capacity of the crane that lifts it, unlike 'in situ' or 'poured in place' concrete, which, as its name implies, is poured into a mould in its final position and, within the limits imposed by thermal expansion, can be built up into great homogeneous masses. The two types of concrete are quite distinctive, and their differences are clearly marked at Marseille: the precast units fairly well made and precise, with joints clear and regular, and the poured concrete rough, jointless and showing the marks of the rough timber moulds. Since anything nailed to the inside of the mould will leave its impress on the finished material, Le Corbusier has played with the concrete near the entrance and by means of the figures of men, the sun and so on, he has set out to explain the ideas that were important to him in the design of this building. On the roof, where the mass of grey concrete might pall, he has set diagonal patterns of coloured tiles into the concrete.

Above, the Villa Stein designed by Le Corbusier in 1928. As a young man, when his only commissions were suburban houses, he often designed them with balconies and blank walls—prototype dwellings to fit into the great blocks he would build one day.

Le Corbusier has said that the glazing at Marseille was not carried out in accordance with his wishes, and his second Unité at Nantes-Rezé (opposite) represents his design. The traditional combination of light source and ventilation has gone; here the glass is fixed shut and the openings are fitted with solid wooden shutters, giving a greater sense of enclosure to the room within than the glass walls of Marseille. 47

The north wall, which receives no sun, is blank except for the fire-escape stairs from the shopping floor. At the south end, the apartments are turned at right angles to obtain maximum sunshine and to house all the flats of non-standard size that were required.

On the exterior, the huge ground-floor stilts and the fact that half of the windows run up through the full height of the two-storey living rooms combine to make the building seem much smaller than it is. In addition, Le Corbusier has tried to relate his vast building to the human scale by making all the dimensions conform to the *modulor*—a rather complex system of measurements designed and patented by him to replace the metre and the foot. *Modulor* dimensions increase on a geometrical and not arithmetical progression; its principal dimensions are related to those of the human body and therefore to man. Man in this context is taken as 6 feet tall, the height of all heroes of English detective novels, according to Le Corbusier, and therefore that of our ideal man. The glazing to the upper half of the two-storey high living room windows is divided into simple rectangles in a rather deadpan manner. Le Corbusier has said that this was carried out in contravention of his instructions while he was away in New York working on the United Nations building, and it was too late to change it on his return. So, in the typically Corbusian way of making a virtue out of setbacks, he decided to deflect the eye from the offending windows by painting the sides to the balconies in bright primary colours. The completed building when seen flat on is the grey colour of concrete, but as the observer moves, the building is seen obliquely and a riot of brilliant colours come into view, giving depth to the façades.

The Marseille building was intended to be cheap, but as so often happens with prototypes, the costs mounted and in the end it proved too expensive for the very people for whom it had been intended. Fortunately, its standards were high enough for middle-class people who could afford economic rents, for the building had become a political football and the subsidy expected was not granted. In later Unités, however, Le Corbusier has shown that he can design within normal cost limits, and the Marseille building was followed two years later by another near Nantes commissioned by the dockers' trade union as housing for their members. Its cost had to fall within the price range of *habitations bon marché* to earn its subsidy, and much of the flamboyance has gone, though the result, if less exciting, is perhaps more easy to live in. Since Nantes, Le Corbusier has completed further Unités at Berlin, Briey-en-Forêt and Firminy.

The Unité at Marseille seen from the north-west.

CHAPTER 2

SEAGRAM BUILDING

Park Avenue at 52nd Street, New York

Mies van der Rohe (or Mies as he is generally known) must be one of the most influential architects who has ever lived. Like Palladio four hundred years earlier, he produced a way of designing buildings notable for its straightforward clarity and which seemed easy to copy. His rectangular, glass-covered towers have been imitated all around the globe, usually crudely and insensitively so that one's eyes, accustomed to seeing bad copies, find it difficult to look at the magnificent originals without being influenced by the inferior replicas. This then is the misfortune of Mies van der Rohe—to be half understood by so many architects and to have half-baked imitations of his buildings constructed in such numbers.

Mies was introduced to building by way of the builder's yard, and not of the architecture school. As a result, a characteristic of his work is that it is always logically buildable; indeed the buildings rely for their architectural impact on the actual means of construction. There is, however, one important exception to this practical rule. This was made in 1919 when, shortly after being demobilised from the German army, Mies designed a series of glass skyscrapers; these were certainly impossible to construct at the time, but they nevertheless gave architecture a powerful new impetus. Unlike Le Corbusier, whose buildings need sunshine to be seen at their best, Mies was raised in northern Europe and to this day he prefers his buildings photographed on days when there is no sunshine, for his is largely an architecture of transparency and of reflection. Mies has said that he had models of his 1919 glass skyscrapers outside his window so that he could study the effect of light on glass buildings.

Mies later settled in Chicago—the city that above all could give him the opportunity he wanted, for there the late 19th-century

tradition of making straightforward architecture out of tall, steel-framed buildings had never wholly died out. In 1950 Mies's first glass and steel towers rose at 860 Lakeshore Drive, overlooking Lake Michigan. Many people have observed how beautiful modern-framed buildings are during construction, when only the frame is standing, square and elegant against the sky. At 860 Lakeshore Drive Mies just built the frame and glazed it, and suddenly all the other tall buildings in the world looked overdressed. But in order to achieve such a simple building, many problems had to be solved, and all the details had to be very carefully worked out. Not surprisingly, when so much is left off, what is left becomes correspondingly more important. This apartment block expressed an architectural concept that was exactly the opposite of that of Le Corbusier's Marseille building; here Mies provides a framework, a background to life, a building in which each occupant can make his own home according to his own tastes and needs and which is not all pre-planned by the architect. Thus the expression of the dwelling on the outside of the building, so important at Marseille, is irrelevant in a Mies building, which in many ways is more like an 18th-century crescent in Bath or a square in Bloomsbury, where individually planned houses were masked behind a regular façade belonging to the whole terrace.

In 1954 the Seagram whisky firm had plans drawn up for a new office building for themselves on Park Avenue. The design was for a typical, run-of-the-mill commercial building. But when Mrs Phyllis Lambert, daughter of Seagram's president and later to become an architect herself, saw the designs she was not impressed and persuaded her father to scrap the design and start again and to allow her to choose the architect. She took this responsibility very seriously, and travelled across the States looking at buildings and interviewing architects. Apparently she found everyone talking of Mies, either for or against, but she found no one as convincing as Mies himself and no buildings as relevant as the towers on Lakeshore Drive. So the task of designing the new Seagram building was given to Mies. In the United States, a licence to practice as an architect is granted by the individual states, and as Mies had no licence to practice in New York he asked his friend and biographer Philip Johnson to be his associate. It is rarely possible to single out to whom credit should be given in a building designed by a partnership, but generally speaking the basic conception of the Seagram building, its structure and skin are by Mies, while Philip Johnson is

Previous pages, left, a steel-and-glass apartment tower at 860 Lakeshore Drive, Chicago, designed by Mies van der Rohe and completed in 1951. The towers were the first of an immaculate series built of metal and glass.

Previous pages, right, the Seagram building, the office tower built by Mies at 375 Park Avenue, New York.

Right, a view of the 90-foot plaza separating the Seagram building from Park Avenue. This plaza, with pools, fountains, paving and trees, made a humdrum site dramatic, and forms a pleasant oasis in a crowded, corridor-like street.

Below, a plan of a typical tower floor showing the lifts, lavatories and service rooms in the centre, with open space on all four sides suitable for subdividing into offices. The long, flat side faces Park Avenue.

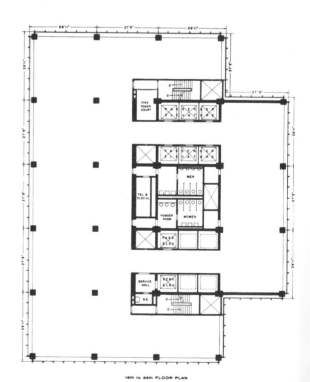

18th to 28th FLOOR PLAN

responsible for the interior work. This collaboration could nearly have ended in disaster, for in 1954 when they were commissioned joint architects, Johnson was producing work which was basically Mies-inspired, but by 1958, when the building was complete, he had changed his style to a dry classicism. Nevertheless, he later disclaimed credit for anything except the interiors.

Unlike most New York firms, Seagram were not primarily interested in making their building profitable, although in fact it did pay a reasonable return on the money invested. Seagram genuinely wanted a fine building and were prepared to pay for it, even to the extent of making a third of the $5-million site an open plaza. Also, at a time when speculative developers were cramming as much rentable space on to their land as possible, Seagram made their building only 60 per cent of the size it could have been. Moreover, at a cost of $45 per square foot it was an expensive undertaking, although not so expensive as some later office buildings in New York and London. But the architects wanted the best and the clients were prepared to pay for it; the result was a luxury building.

Above, a night shot that clearly reveals the structural frame of the building. The luminous ceiling of the perimeter offices is controlled centrally so that the building, as seen from the outside, appears to be evenly lit.

Opposite, the base of the tower seen from the Racquet Club on the other side of Park Avenue. 55

The clients, Joseph E. Seagram and Sons, wanted to occupy part of the building themselves and to let off the rest to tenants. In addition, they expected that indefinable quality known as 'prestige', which adds status to a building and thus to its occupants. Obviously too there is considerable advertising value in the whole of New York talking about, 'The Seagram building', while sensational colour pages in such magazines as *Time* and *Life* are also welcome publicity.

The site occupies half a midtown New York block. (No opportunity here for the super-block planning of Rockefeller Center or the Chase Manhattan Bank on Wall Street.) But the site faces Park Avenue and is directly opposite the Racquet Club, a pleasant classical pastiche dating from the turn of the century; diagonally opposite is Lever House, a splendid building finished a few years before Seagram was begun. Lever is a very glassy building, which owed much to the Miesian projects of 1919 and started its architects, Skidmore, Owings and Merrill, on a long series of immaculate buildings for American business corporations, such as the Upjohn Building at Kalamazoo (described in Chapter 8).

A characteristic of a modern office building is that it is meant for nobody in particular; office requirements change, tenants come and go, departments grow and shrink continually, and even in New York they cannot afford to build a new building every time such a change occurs. Thus an efficient office building is one that provides heat, light, ventilation, outlets for electricity, telephones and all the other gadgetry of office communications but does not fix any of the internal walls. The building goes up with a core of lifts, stairs, lavatories and so on, but the rest is rented out as anonymous, but well-serviced space. The tenant then comes in and puts up his own walls and partitions, all of which can be moved whenever necessary. These may or may not be designed by the architect for the whole building. But although the architect may not be responsible for the partitioning of the inside, he must consider the possible position of partitions when designing the mullions, the structure and the service core. This rather unspecific relationship to the activities inside the building is very much in line with Mies's approach to architecture. He wrote:

'My concept and approach to the Seagram Building was no different from any other building that I might build. My idea, or better, "direction", in which I go is toward a clear structure

Above, a view along East 53rd Street, showing the Seagram building in close-up. The metal work is bronze, and the glass is tinted a similar colour, so blinds, curtains and so on seen through the windows also appear brown.

Right, looking up the tower through one of the glass-covered side canopies.

56

and construction—this applies not to any one problem but to all architectural problems which I approach. I am, in fact, completely opposed to the idea that a specific building should have an individual character—rather, a universal character which has been determined by the total problem which architecture must strive to solve.

On the Seagram Building, since it was to be built in New York, and since it was the first major office building which I was to build, I asked for two types of advice for the development of the plans. One, the best real-estate advice as to the types of desirable rentable space and, two, professional advice regarding the New York City Building Code. With my direction established and, with these advisers, it was then only a matter of hard work.'

Mies set his building back 90 feet to form a 'plaza' between the tower and the road; this idea has now become commonplace, but at the time was an unheard-of extravagance. From this plaza the building rises sheer for 520 feet, a crisp, clean tower of beautiful materials and workmanship. Without the financial restrictions that Mies had experienced at Lakeshore Drive and with a client who wanted the best and an associate who had a penchant for the luxurious, it was decided to clad the building in bronze. So while other New York skyscrapers became slicker and more silver and more shiny, Seagram stood out very dark, the colour of an old penny; in the words of the English architect Peter Smithson ' . . . everything else now looks like a jumped-up supermarket'.

The structure is of bolted steelwork, with columns 27 feet 9 inches apart in both directions. These columns only take vertical loads; all wind loads are taken down a braced construction next to the lifts. The steel frame is covered with concrete as fire protection, and this concrete is faced with bronze. Bronze extrusions, $4\frac{1}{2}$ inches by 6 inches are fastened to the face of the building as mullions to receive the glass and any internal partitions that may be needed. Floor slabs, where they show on the outside of the building are faced with 'Muntz metal', similar to bronze in colour but more suitable for use in flat sheets. To emphasise this bronze look, a brown-coloured glass is used in all the windows. This makes life more pleasant for those inside by cutting down the glare of the sky; it also avoids the messy outside appearance of many all-glass buildings in which the interior decoration—venetian blinds and so on—are clearly seen.

58 The architects took two further steps to keep the building looking

Above, a reception area in the Seagram offices. Materials are luxurious, original works of art abound, and everything is studiously underplayed. The chairs and tables were designed by Mies thirty years earlier.

Opposite, one of the side entrances that provide covered access to taxis on wet days when crossing the plaza would mean a soaking. The side entrance also serves The Four Seasons Restaurant.

Left, The Four Seasons Restaurant in the projecting back wing of the building, lavishly designed by Philip Johnson using furniture designed by Mies.

simple: first they made the venetian blinds so that they could only stop in the up or down positions and fixed the louvres of the blinds at 45 degrees so that their presence would be minimised when seen from the street; secondly they put all the lights around the perimeter of the building on a separate circuit, which tenants could not control. At night, then, the building is seen as a rectangular frame, not the random patchwork of lights dictated by the number of people working late on that particular evening.

One of the reasons why the structural frame at 860 Lakeshore Drive appears so strong is that the columns are in the outer skin and show on the exterior. At Seagram, on the other hand, there is an air-conditioning system, which needs pipes on the perimeter running outside the columns. So unlike 860, which was a frame-and-fill system, Seagram has a curtain wall with the skin held outside the columns, which show only at ground level or at night when the building is lit from within. This suppression of the structural frame gives the building a bland air when viewed from the front, but the

The Bacardi office building in Mexico City, completed four years after Seagram. It closely resembles the lower two floors of the earlier building, for Mies believes in universal solutions to architectural problems.

6-inch projection of all the mullions makes the skin come alive as soon as it is seen in perspective.

Just as the outside is sheathed in bronze and brown glass so the inside is equally luxurious. The vertical stack containing the lifts is covered with travertine—a cream-coloured marble quarried in the hills of Rome—the ceiling of the entrance lobby is of grey mosaic set in black cement, and its floor is of granite while the floors in offices and lift lobbies are carpeted.

The air-conditioning plant is on the top of the tower, surrounded by a high parapet of bronze louvres. These louvres are fitted to mullions similar to those supporting the glazing below so that vertical elements run up the face of the building without a break. The conditioned air from this roof-top plant is delivered to the offices by units running around the perimeter of the building. These units, only 11 inches high, separate the furniture and people inside the building from the glass skin. (The glass is floor to ceiling, and at 400 feet above Park Avenue people might suffer from vertigo while furniture against the glass would spoil the building's neat and tidy appearance on the outside.)

Lighting around the outer 11 feet 6 inches of the building is provided by a luminous ceiling. In this system—which makes the tower so dramatic at night—the lights are above the ceiling and diffused by a continuous membrane at ceiling level. (This kind of lighting gives a shadowless light, which is theoretically good for working but in fact is rather boring. But in a building that is entirely glazed such a system is necessary to prevent the ceiling from seeming dark in contrast to the light coming through the glass.) In the entrance and the lift lobbies recessed incandescent lights are used; these are deeply sunk in black recesses so that the source of light is almost invisible. Similar lights are used to illuminate the fine collection of paintings and tapestries Phyllis Lambert chose for Seagram's own offices.

Seen from Park Avenue, the Seagram building is so straightforward that even Mies's detractors were impressed. But around the back are low buildings that are anything but clear and even Mies's students are at a loss to know what to think. Had the master fumbled? Had he just done what he could with the accommodation that would not fit into the tower? Or was it an attempt to make a relationship with the low buildings adjoining? Mies is a man of few words and has not commented, but Philip Johnson put into the low part of the building one of the most luxurious restaurants ever designed— the Four Seasons—which uses furniture designed by Mies twenty-five years earlier. It has a rich, glamorous, slightly playboy character that could never have been dreamed up by Mies, who views architecture with an almost religious seriousness.

A further expression of his search for general as opposed to particular solutions to architectural problems was built by Mies in Mexico City in 1961—a small office building that looks as if the entrance lobby and one floor of the Seagram building had been made into a separate structure. The client and the climate were different, but to Mies these points were of minor significance compared with all the factors that were the same. At a time when American architects are constantly seeking self-expression and a new fashion each week, the continued, deliberate, unhurried development of Mies towards ever clearer solutions has put the rest of the profession to shame and the elegance and skill with which his buildings are constructed make other architecture—except perhaps that of his own students—look amateurish.

A night photograph showing the Seagram tower as a shaft of light, making the surrounding buildings look uninhabited in comparison.

CHAPTER 3

CROWN HALL

Campus of the Illinois Institute of Technology,
South State Street, Chicago, Illinois

Mies van der Rohe was the last director of the Bauhaus, that progressive school of art, architecture and allied subjects that flourished in Germany in the 1920s and finally closed under Nazi pressure in 1933. After it had shut down, Mies found no opportunity to teach and little opportunity to build in a Germany that was demanding a nationalistic architecture, for the Nazis were totally opposed to modern design for buildings. In 1938 Mies settled in the United States, and after the years of enforced idleness he threw himself enthusiastically into the task of teaching and building.

Mies was invited to Chicago to head the architecture school at Armour Institute (later the Illinois Institute of Technology). He was also commissioned to design the new campus on slum-clearance land to the south of the Chicago Loop. Mies realised that the campus would take a long time to build, so he did not design all the buildings at once, but drew a grid of 12-foot squares over the site plan; he then filled in the squares with buildings whenever they were required. So much for the site layout, now what of the buildings themselves? The steel frame had been invented in Chicago. It was a modern, machine-made material, it was cheap and it enabled the construction of frames for every conceivable kind of building. Its steeliness too could be emphasised by painting it black. And so the campus grew, with buildings that, whatever function they served, had a structure of a black steel frame in squares of 12 feet or multiples of 12 feet. Thus the Institute could develop at its own pace, without ever having a half-finished look, and could continue to grow and change indefinitely. Because each building is a complete design in itself, it looks fine on its own, but when grouped together, the whole scheme comes together as one great piece of architecture, for the 12-foot

Student discussion in Crown Hall. Because the room is so large, several groups may be talking at once without disturbing one another.

grid, shared by all the buildings and the spaces in between, ties them into a coherent whole. At last it seemed that here was not just another good modern building, but a whole area of the city designed as an ensemble by a great modern architect. Unfortunately nearly twenty years after the arrival of Mies (when the campus was about half finished) a new administration at I.I.T. decided, in the name of variety, to give sections of the work to other architects. The students ran a front-page protest, but without success, so the Mies work at I.I.T. remains a fraction of a great might-have-been.

Mies is fond of saying that there is a hierarchy of building types, and that 'not every building is a cathedral'. By this he means that while every building should be well-designed, some require, in

varying degrees, an emotional loading. In a medieval English village, for example, the church and the tithe barn might be of similar size and built in a similar way with similar materials. But while the tithe barn is a functional building, the church is given a spiritual value by the skill of its designer. In answer to this, one might well ask, which buildings today have this emotional load to carry? What is the cathedral of the 20th century? For Mies, with his more than monastic dedication to his profession, one answer is clearly the building where architecture is taught. Thus Crown Hall, the building where architects are trained, is the 'cathedral' of the I.I.T. campus. The other buildings are beautifully designed, but prosaic. Crown Hall is on a grander scale by reason of its 18-foot ceiling height; its precise symmetry also makes it a more self-conscious work of architecture. To use an analogy made by Mies, the other buildings speak good prose, but Crown Hall speaks poetry.

One of the cornerstones of Mies's architectural philosophy is the concept of 'universal space'. By this he means space not permanently dedicated to one specific use. Mies had grown up in the centuries-old European tradition of heavy masonry buildings serving societies that changed very slowly. In these circumstances, architects had always closely tailored the design of a room to the function it was to serve, whether dining room, chapel or class-room. This approach was not only practical but part of an architectural tradition, which measured buildings' success by the extent to which they 'expressed their function'. In middle age Mies found himself in America, in a technical institute where new developments could make buildings out of date before they were finished and the comfortable old European attitude was called in question. So Mies rethought his ideas and designed his American buildings to be as unspecific as is reasonable. Indeed his office buildings and apartment buildings are very similar and could easily be converted from one use to the other—a practical idea when one considers how many private houses in, say, London have been unsatisfactorily converted into offices.

Yet having largely eliminated function as a form-giver what have we left with which to create an architecture? Only the structure and the outside skin, for only these will last the life of the building if decade after decade the inside is changed continually to satisfy every new demand that arises. And so it is on refining the skin and the bones that Mies has concentrated his intense, rational search for perfection.

In order to make the space at Crown Hall as general and undefined

A general view of Crown Hall showing the two wide flights of steps leading to the entrance. The surrounding trees when in leaf would keep out some of the hot Chicago sun.

as possible, the structure has been pulled outside the building. Any inside structure would have tended to dictate the subdivisions of the space in the interior and make it more specific. The structure, thus exteriorised, becomes a most powerful visual element. The building not only has to house the students but also to explain the nature of architecture in such clear and forcible terms that they may never have the excuse that they did not understand. The structure is almost bridge-like in scale, and encloses a space 220 feet long and 120 feet wide without interior supports. The main roof is suspended from four great steel plate girders placed 60 feet apart and supported at each end on a steel column. Each 120-foot long girder was built up in the fabricating shop in two halves so that 60-foot sections were brought to the site, joined and hoisted into position. The roof spans 60 feet between the girders and at each end cantilevers 20 feet beyond them; this cantilever reduces the stresses in the adjacent 60-foot spans. As in so much Miesian work good architecture and good engineering go hand in hand.

So much for the bones, now what of the skin? A visitor to Mies's office in Chicago will see that a quarter of its area is workshop space. Here architects make models of the buildings they are designing—models that are changed and remade until the general form of the building is finalised. Then a full size mock-up of part of the skin is made and worked on—a mullion added here, a sill raised a few inches there—until Mies and his designers are satisfied. The process may take months. Le Corbusier can use his *modulor* to help him with the proportions of his buildings, Buckminster Fuller may use complex mathematics, but for Mies there are no props, no short-cuts, only endless patience and a tireless capacity for taking pains and exercising his judgement. The atmosphere, with Mies in his wheel-chair, puffing at his cigar and asking an assistant to make slight alterations to the mock-up under consideration, has been compared to that of an operating theatre where a great surgeon is performing a revolutionary operation for the first time.

The skin finally chosen for Crown Hall divides each 60-foot bay into six 10-foot wide spaces with five vertical mullions, each an I-beam similar to the columns but smaller. The lower part of the room is glazed with sand-blasted glass and above this there is clear glass to the ceiling with venetian blinds kept permanently lowered. This horizontal division between clear and obscure glass occurs just above head height and so gives a recognisable human scale to the whole building and enables the entrance doors to be neatly integrated

Left, a general view of a draughting area from the entrance. The low screen is not permanent and is used to display student work and to define areas for meeting.

Below, general view showing the great size of the interior. Note the ceiling hung from the girders above the roof so that no internal supports are needed.

An elegant metal rail surrounds the raised terrace at the entrance, left. This terrace, of steel with a travertine top, forms a gathering place for students and takes the visitor up to the main-floor level in easy stages.

'I think this is the clearest structure we have done,' said the architect. As can be seen, right, the black-painted steel frame is completely filled with glass so that no solid wall conflicts with the clarity of Mies's structure.

Below, a plan of the main level. The central area is a great exhibition space, so that the many visitors who come to Crown Hall can see the students at work.

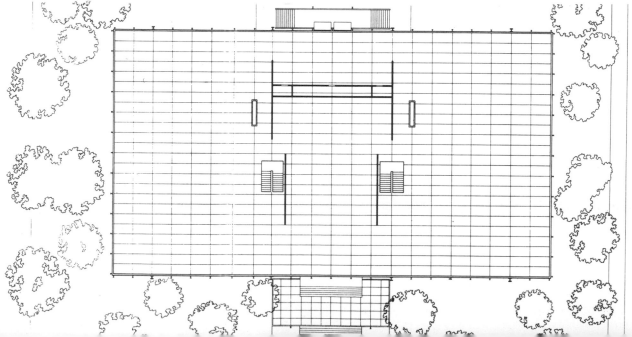

into the design of the skin. Such logic in making a building, and making architecture out of the actual members of its construction, leads to simple building and to economy, and at the cost of 78 cents a cubic foot Crown Hall is an astonishingly cheap building.

The building is planned to include air conditioning. The budget did not allow for this to be installed initially, but ductwork has been put in for its operation in the future. The diffusers for this are circular and fit somewhat unhappily into a ceiling of square acoustic tiles and rectangular light fittings. Obviously, in such an open building the ceiling is very important visually, but the budget was tight so fittings could not be specially designed and in 1955 the standard range was limited. Mechanical plant for ventilation is in the basement and this is connected to the intake on the roof by two ducts, which inevitably have to go right through the building and this contravenes the universal-space, clear-span idea. However, Mies has detailed them very carefully, so that they are played down as much as possible. They are painted white, are recessed at the top and set well away from any structural line.

Although at first sight the building appears to contain just one great room, it is in fact a two-storey building. The lower floor, sunk to a semi-basement level, houses the Institute of Design, a school of industrial design and photography, which traces its ancestry back to the Bauhaus. Mies has been heavily criticised for relegating this internationally famous Institute to a basement; it has even been suggested that he deliberately put them underground because he did not like their teaching methods! The real reason is more prosaic. Building regulations in Chicago would not allow the construction of a two-storey building in steelwork unless the steel was wrapped in a fireproof casing (steel rapidly loses strength when heated); but they would permit a single-storey building with a basement. Mies's great-space concept needed uncased steel, so the Institute of Design was sunk into the ground just far enough to qualify as a basement. In fact, it was high enough to have a 3-foot strip of window, and since the Institute of Design consists largely of workshops, the premises provided are really quite acceptable.

Not surprisingly, Mies lavished most love and care on his architecture school—a great space, 220 feet by 120 feet, with a sense of patrician, machine-made calm. The few divisions that do exist (apart from the service ducts) are only 6 feet high, so from anywhere in the room the sky can be seen on all four sides. Students work, hold discussions and are criticised by their tutors; staff work at their tables, people come and go and look at exhibitions, all within one great space, which is so large that individual sounds are lost. Thus the occupants can go about their business and in no way damage the harmony of the whole. (Educationally it is claimed to

Far left, a view from above showing the four great trusses from which the roof is suspended. In the centre of the roof is the penthouse containing the mechanical equipment for ventilating the building. Beyond can be seen the surrounding buildings of Chicago's seedy South side being demolished to make room for the growing I.I.T. campus.

For a hundred years, men in Chicago had built with steel, but it was traditionally covered up to look like something else. As can be seen in the view, centre, Mies's great breakthrough was to let the steel stand on its own, and lovingly to profile it and join it so that it acquired a nobility comparable to the materials of the buildings of the past.

Below, Crown Hall in a snowy landscape. The windows of the semi-basement housing the Institute of Design are below the main-floor level.

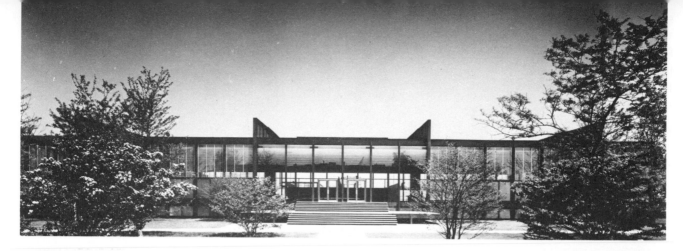

Most of the early modern buildings were deliberately asymmetrical, because symmetry was felt to have associations with the old classical architecture. Mies is less concerned with such issues, and, as demonstrated in the view at the top of the page, the plan and structure of the Crown Hall are both logically symmetrical. So, in spite of the materials, the building has some of the feel of a classical temple.

In the dusk shot, above, the classical quality and the elegance of the steelwork are emphasised by the lights inside, which throw the skin into silhouette. The regular pattern of lights set in the ceiling further reinforces the basic idea of the great roof slab, hovering above the occupants.

Left, a construction photograph showing the raised floor in position and the steelwork being erected. Two of the great plate-girders supporting the roof are in position; the other two are assembled complete and are waiting to be lifted on to their supporting columns.

be beneficial for the student to be able to see everything that goes on in the school.) The 6-foot-high oak screens divide off a central area for waiting and exhibitions. The placing of these screens, like that of the entrances and the service ducts, is symmetrical, for the structure of the building and the circulation patterns of the people inside it are symmetrical, and the symmetry is emphasised by omitting the venetian blinds and the sand-blasted glass from the central bay of the building. These variations, though minor in themselves, nevertheless give a very different quality of light to the exhibition areas, which have sunlight and an uninterrupted view out, whereas the work areas in the rest of the room are lit by a more diffuse light, which the venetian blinds bounce right across the building.

Crown Hall was opened in April 1956, and Mies van der Rohe, ever the master of understatement, said of the completed building: 'I think that this is the clearest structure we have done.'

Below, an early drawing by Mies showing internal columns. These were omitted in later designs, since the beams above the roof made a clear span possible.

Bottom, a model of Crown Hall. Just as the students occupying the completed building make models of their designs, so the assistants in Mies's office make models to refine and improve their own projects.

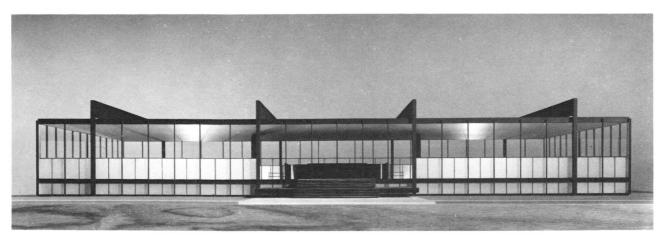

CHAPTER 4

THE PALACE OF LABOUR

Italia '61 Exhibition, Turin

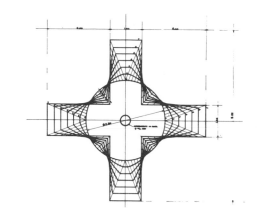

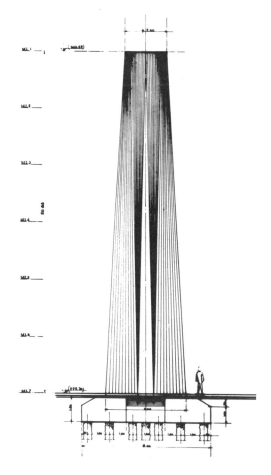

Pier Luigi Nervi was not trained as an architect; he graduated in engineering at the University of Bologna in 1913 and then worked for a firm of building contractors, later becoming part-owner and director of the company. He has rarely been commissioned by a patron to build a fine building but he has obtained work by the 'design and tender' competition system prevalent in Italy, whereby the requirements of a proposed building are published and the contract awarded to the company that submits the design with the lowest price. Such a background might be expected to produce a tough, commercially minded practical man with a philistine attitude to aesthetics. Instead it produced, in Nervi, a fine designer, who has built some of the greatest buildings in postwar Europe. It has been said that the Renaissance ideal of the universal man is no longer relevant and that this is the age of the expert. Yet besides being a leading expert in the field of concrete engineering, Nervi is also a successful business man, has written books on aesthetics and held a Harvard Professorship of Poetry.

Although he may be a man of many parts, Nervi is a complete man and the different facets of his character are closely interlocked. Because he is an engineer who has had to earn his living by designing economically, he sees the whole history of architecture as the development of structure and practical building skills, with the parts played by social conditions and aesthetic theory relegated to positions of secondary importance. Nervi sees the history of architecture as the evolution of building technique, with less efficient systems becoming extinct and flexible ones adapting to new conditions. To him the architecture of the ancient Egyptians and Greeks was
76 that of closely spaced columns because they used large stones

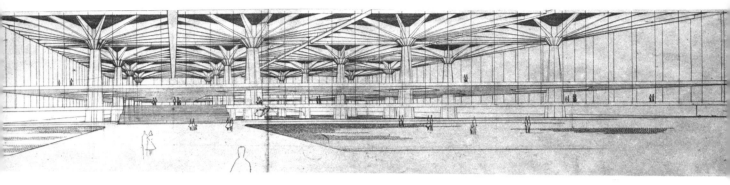

spanning from column to column, and there was an obvious limit to the size of stone they could lift into position. Architecture did not change until the Romans' use of crude concrete made possible the 80-foot spans of their baths and the great walls needed to buttress them dictated the form of the plan. In medieval times, the slave labour that built the massive structures of the Romans was no longer available, so builders had to learn, by trial and error, how to build ribbed vaults out of small stones, and flying buttresses to take the load and thrust in the great cathedrals. Nervi has unbounded admiration for these medieval builders who, he believes, came to understand the nature of equilibrium intuitively. He points out that the mouldings on the vaulting of King's College Chapel in Cambridge follow the lines of principal stress and produce a structure not unlike Nervi's mezzanine at the Palace of Labour. In the 19th century the old intuitive tradition was replaced by scientific technology. This was both a gain and a loss: the humanising agent of collective experience, of pushing the limits a little further than your predecessor, was lost, but the gain was a new world of opportunities, missed for a while by the architects but seized by the engineers Brunel, Eiffel and Roebling. The calculation by formula of these early engineers has been extended in our own time by computers, which means that the engineer is no longer tied to easily calculable forms, and by model testing, which enables the engineer to determine the stress in forms not yet able to be analysed mathematically.

As might be expected of a man with such an approach to history, Nervi sees the architectural problem of our time as that of choosing and building the right structure. This he believes is the basis from which a talented designer can create a powerful work. But if the structure is not right, all is lost, for, says Nervi, 'There does not

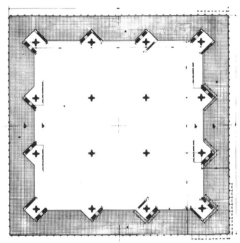

Top, a drawing showing the building as its designers hoped it would look—open and transparent with its structure strongly visible. As it turned out, the closing-in of the lower floors and the sun shades in front of the glazing have made it much more solid-looking.

Above, a plan of the building with the mezzanine gallery shown hatched.

Opposite, engineer's drawings of one of the sixteen concrete columns supporting the roof. The top of the column is an 8-foot diameter circle, the base is an 18-foot cross; the form of the column is made by linking these two profiles with straight lines.

77

exist, either in the past or the present, a work of architecture which is accepted and recognised as excellent from the aesthetic point of view which is not also excellent from the technical point of view.' Nervi will admit to being not quite sure why this should be so, but he believes that the eye is satisfied when a building looks stable, finds it vulgar if its parts are too heavy, and so expects it to be well engineered in order to look stable but not weighty. Thus he admires the beauty of bridges and aircraft because they have the 'truthfulness' architects should strive for. In his own words, 'The expressive efficiency of these creations is in perfect accord with the laws of physics'.

The first Nervi building to demonstrate his philosophy in a clear and unmistakable way was the stadium at Florence designed in 1928. This stadium was elegantly built in reinforced concrete with a magnificent curved roof cantilevering 17 metres over the seats, and some delicate curved concrete staircases, which were incredibly

Opposite, top, a construction photograph show-ing the 65-feet-high concrete columns, with the steel beams radiating out to support the roof.

Opposite, bottom, an exterior view showing the sun shades that protect the glass walls from the Italian sun. The mullions are 70 feet high and under considerable wind load, so they are braced with vertical fins.

Left, strip light along the steel roof girders reveal the structure dramatically at night. Built for the Italia '61 exhibition, the Palace of Labour has all the flamboyance and drama associated with exhibition buildings since the Crystal Palace.

Below, a photograph of a corner column taken as the building nears completion. The tapering forms of the concrete column and the steel roof beams respond to the stresses within them.

light and elegant for the time. The first part of the stadium was completed in 1930 and at that time the modern movement in archi-tecture was becoming an international force and books on the sub-ject began to be published on a large scale. However, there were not all that many good buildings to write about and the new Florence stadium was taken up as the building of the moment and was illustrated alongside the buildings of Le Corbusier and Walter Gropius as a modern movement classic. Yet until he was 'discovered' by the architects in 1930, Nervi's motivation had been very different from that of his discoverers, and the stadium at Florence might well have been built just as it is if there had been no modern movement in architecture. However, Nervi was brought into the circle of modern architects and there has been much influence both ways ever since.

In the postwar years, Nervi's fame among architects brought him a series of commissions for buildings designed in collaboration with famous architects: the Pirelli building in Milan with Gio Ponti, the UNESCO building in Paris with Marcel Breuer and Bernard Zehr-fuss and the Australia Square Tower in Sydney with Harry Seidler. But the greatest of his postwar buildings are a series of exhibition halls in Turin, culminating in the Palazzo del Lavoro completed in 1961.

It was decided to hold an exhibition to commemorate a hundred years of Italian unity, in which one of the buildings was to house

exhibits concerning the contribution of labour. Turin was chosen as the site for the exhibition because it was there that the unity of Italy was proclaimed in 1861, with Rome as the new capital of the whole country. The schedule allowed only seventeen months to design and build a structure of some 485,000 square feet, and to make life even more difficult, the competition conditions required that the exhibition hall should be capable of conversion into a technical school when the exhibition was over!

The design and price submitted by Nervi and his son Antonio won the competition, largely because their building could be erected quickly. As had happened with the Crystal Palace 110 years earlier, shortage of time forced the exhibition organisers to accept a new form of structure in order to cut down building time. The Nervi design consisted of 16 mushrooms, each completely separate so that no part of the structure needed to wait for any other part to be complete. Some of Nervi's rivals had proposed roofing the exhibition space with one great clear span, but the assessors doubted their ability to complete in time.

All Nervi's earlier buildings had been in reinforced concrete, which he described as 'the most fertile, ductile and complete construction process that mankind has yet found'. Here, however, he realised that a concrete roof for his building would be slow to build. So, always the pragmatist, he roofed his building in steel, which he nevertheless submitted to the same discipline as the concrete supports: both change their profile as the stresses within them change, not only because this is sound engineering practice, but also because of Nervi's belief that the form of a structure should manifest the stresses within it.

Each of the 16 mushrooms consists of a concrete stem 65 feet high and a steel roof 125 feet square. These mushrooms are divided by 6-foot gaps. These gaps serve two purposes: they are glazed to let daylight down into the centre of a 525-foot-square building and also show clearly that each mushroom is free-standing and does not rely on its neighbour for support. The concrete column is circular, with an 8-foot diameter at the top where it joins the steelwork; at the bottom the column is in the form of an 18-foot cross, which is better able to resist bending stresses induced by wind. The shape of the column shaft is formed by linking the circle and the cross by straight lines. The use of straight lines is important, not only aesthetically, but also because it enables the formwork into which the concrete is poured to be made out of straight pieces of timber.

Five horizontal recesses in the concrete column, above, mark the day-work joints; the concrete between each pair of these joints is poured at one time and the groove serves to hide any slight change in colour or alignment.

Opposite, two mushrooms of the Palace of Labour showing the concrete posts supporting the steel roof structure.

81

These columns are the most prominent elements in the building, and because it is not possible to patch faulty concrete satisfactorily, great care was taken with the formwork. This was made up of six pieces fitting one on top of the other, each piece framed in steel with two layers of wood as a lining. A $1\frac{1}{2}$-inch-square recess was also made in the column where the different pieces of formwork met to disguise any variation between concrete poured in the various sections. Each of the 16 columns took ten days to cast, using the same formwork. The magnificent umbrella of steel on top of the columns consists of 20 steel cantilevers, each one tapering as the load on it diminishes.

The entire building is clad in glass. The mullions supporting the glass skin are 70 feet high and under considerable horizontal pressure when the wind blows on the glass. Nervi has therefore placed vertical fins outside each mullion to take the wind load and these fins are thick in the centre where the bending moment is great and thin at the ends where it is less. On the sunny sides of the building there are metal louvres to prevent the building from getting too hot in summer.

Around the perimeter is a gallery providing a mezzanine floor. This was to house the smaller exhibits, for as well as the central Italian exhibition there were minor displays by the U.S.A., U.S.S.R.,

Far left, top, the exhibition building in use, the great structure a background to the displays and exhibits commemorating a hundred years of Italian unity.

Far left, bottom, a roof-level view showing the upper level of exhibition space in the gallery.

Centre, escalators passing a corner column; stairs, escalators and the face of the gallery are set at 45 degrees to the main structure to emphasise their separateness.

Tunisia, Switzerland, Denmark, Finland, Germany, Japan, France and Britain. The mezzanine has its own constructional system, and is held clear of the main columns so as not to appear supported by them. The mezzanine construction is one used many times by Nervi— concrete poured into *ferro-cimento* formwork. Concrete is usually poured into moulds of wood or steel, and because of the nature of these materials, beams are usually made in straight lines even though this form may not be the most satisfactory in engineering terms. Nervi invented a material made by plastering cement on wire mesh, called *ferro-cimento*, which he used for formwork because it can readily be made into curved forms. The beam structure of the mezzanine is therefore formed of curved members, following the lines of stress in the concrete and producing a beautiful elegant ceiling. To further emphasise the difference between the main structure of the mushrooms and the subsidiary structure with its curved beams, Nervi placed them at 45 degrees on each other, so circulation routes—staircases and escalators—leading to the mezzanine pass diagonally across the main columns.

The structure is by far the most impressive feature. The details— and fire-escape stairs, the doorways, the fittings—seem to have just happened. As an engineer Nervi knows how to build great structures, but by missing the training of an architect he was never taught to notice the little things that add so much to the quality of a building. Nervi, like Buckminster Fuller, gets the big things right and is ham-fisted with the small things. This is why they are both at their most successful in buildings requiring a very large space, where the details are less important than the overall structural idea and where the form of the building can demonstrate what Nervi calls 'the existence of an unpredictable and not easily explained rapport between technical correctness and aesthetic expression'.

When the turnstiles are closed and the crowds have gone, exhibition buildings are sorry places, and the Palazzo del Lavoro is no exception. The monorail that brought the throngs of visitors is rust streaked, its station choked with weeds and surrounded by barbed wire. In the building itself, the mezzanine has been converted into a Centre for Advanced Technical Studies for overseas students. This conversion involved partitioning the space below and above the mezzanine floor and adding a second, higher mezzanine to the great detriment of the proportions inside and out. The great space with its 16 columns remains, unused and empty, save for the odd

student taking a short-cut from one class-room to another.

CHAPTER 5

UNION TANK CAR DOME

Baton Rouge, Louisiana

Buckminster Fuller is a creative oddball who has become the technological conscience of the modern movement in architecture. For while most modern architects talk about bringing the technology of the aircraft and space industries into building, Fuller alone actually does so. An engineer who recognises no professional boundaries, he has designed cars and aircraft, made maps and furniture in addition to concentrating on his central preoccupation of designing buildings. But although the subject may vary, his approach is always the same: achieving the maximum performance from the minimum of materials, and he has ruthlessly pursued this aim wherever it might lead him. In building, this attitude has led to the construction of domes because no other shape offers such a favourable ratio between space enclosed and surface area. When discussing a building, typical Fuller questions are 'how much does it weigh?' or 'how many cubic feet of container space are needed to transport it to the site?'. Such questions are not asked in conventional architectural criticism, but to Fuller they are fundamental since they are an indication of the energy input, which must be compared with performance output. Fuller believes that in our 20th-century democratic society the possibility of the good life for any man depends on the possibility of realising it for all men. So as a basis for his work, he has prepared an inventory of all the materials in the world and all the available energy sources; then, by relating these constants to the number of people, he can find out how much we can each have without being greedy. From this powerful statistical strongpoint, he constantly attacks the building industry for its failure to make use of 'the direct application of world living standards'.

Fuller was for a time part-owner of the Stockade Building System,

Left, the model of the 1927 first Dymaxion house, technically far advanced of any house yet constructed. The central mast houses all the mechanical services, and the floors are suspended from it on wire rigging. The house could be set down anywhere, for it was to be independent of all main services.

Fuller's preoccupation with enclosing the maximum volume with the minimum of material led him to perfect the dome structure, and to produce buildings so light that they can be delivered by helicopter, as in the photograph below.

a building firm producing a clever, but not particularly sophisticated, form of construction. However, a major influence on his life was the tragic death of his young daughter in a post-First World War epidemic. Fuller believed that the epidemic and consequently his daughter's death were caused by bad housing conditions, and he left the world of conventional building and conventional business forever, to devote his life and his tremendous energy to an almost single-handed struggle to apply the advantages of sophisticated technology to the housing of people, particularly the underprivileged.

In 1927 Buckminster Fuller designed his first Dymaxion house. (Dymaxion is a word invented from dynamic and maximum.) Forty years later no house has been built that even begins to approach it technically—a severe indictment of the building industry when one considers the revolutionary advances made in most other fields during the same period. The first Dymaxion house is suspended from a central Duralumin (an aluminium alloy) mast. From this mast hang a sun roof and two hexagonal decks, held in place by steel tension cables like the rigging of a yacht. The outside of the house is covered with double-pane vacuum units, which can be opaque or transparent as required. Doors are pneumatic and fold silently, controlled by photoelectric cells. Beds are pneumatic, and so is the floor, which is thus quiet to walk on. The central mast

86

houses all the mechanical services. Air is drawn in from the top of the mast, cleaned and humidified, warmed or cooled and distributed into the rooms; light also comes from the central mast and is diffused by prisms and reflected by mirrors into the area in which is it needed. This is a rather clumsy arrangement, but the concentration of services, including light sources, into the mast was carried through to an obsessive degree. Cooking, laundering and cleaning were totally mechanised, bathing was by 'fog gun'. Every domestic chore had been anticipated and largely eliminated. The house was designed to be independent of all mains services, for Fuller has said that 'our communications systems and transportation systems have graduated from wire to wireless, pave to paveless, pipe to pipeless; we must graduate our dwelling trends in like terms'. Within the central mast garbage is consumed, electricity generated, human waste is packaged, water is purified and recirculated. Internal partitioning is largely by means of mechanical units, for Fuller has said that partitions are 'a make-do, like socialism. When there is not enough to go round, both provide an arbitrary subdivision of inadequacy. But competent design can always provide adequacy.'

The cost of the first Dymaxion house was expressed in typical Fuller terms: a five-room house weighs 6000 lb and could retail in 1927, assuming mass-production, for 25 cents a lb. (This seems reasonable in comparison with 22 cents a lb for a car of the same year.) All this still seems to belong to a fantasy world because our thinking about houses is so conservative, although none of the Dymaxion's features would seem unreasonable in an aeroplane, and many would seem primitive in a spacecraft. In 1928 Buckminster Fuller offered plans and patents of the house to the American Institute of Architects; they were rejected with scorn. Yet in 1959 the same Institute elected him an honorary member—an example of the shift in establishment thinking and a confirmation of Fuller's statement that it takes a quarter of a century for an idea to be accepted.

The depression came; industry did not tool up for the Dymaxion house and Fuller went on to develop his domes. The pursuit of maximum output for minimum input leads inevitably to the dome, since it is a very stable shape structurally and, as has already been pointed out, encloses the maximum volume with the minimum of surface and hence with the least quantity of material. Fuller developed the geometry of the surface to give him increasingly greater strength for increasingly less material. The beautiful economy of the

Mr and Mrs Buckminster Fuller in their home at Carbondale, Illinois. Never one to experiment on other people, Fuller lives in one of his domes, and has a high, open room to reveal as much as possible of the domical form.

domes Fuller built was at once apparent. In his own terms, he had made a dramatic breakthrough. Never before had it been possible to enclose so much with so little. The disadvantage was that so few of the problems architects have to tackle in an increasingly urbanised society are suitably answered by the dome shape. So Fuller domes were built as exhibition buildings, as art exhibits and as university experiments for years until the military authorities discovered that they were an economical alternative to the tent. In the late 1950s the U.S. Marines ordered the mass-production of domes, which, according to its logistics branch, 'are 3 per cent of the weight of the previous solution, 6 per cent of the packaged volume, 14 per cent of the cost and less than 1 per cent of the erection man-hours'. Military demands for the domes increased, different types and sizes were put into production, and they now house U.S. Marines and their equipment from Antarctica to the DEW (distant early warning) line across northern Canada where all the installations are in Fuller-designed polyester domes.

At this point the tragic element in Fuller's career can be clearly seen. The young idealist, appalled by the housing conditions of most of the world's citizens, had set out with great resolve to tackle the problem by using advanced techniques, clear ideas, mass-production. Twenty-five years later, his impact on housing was negligible while his ideas were enthusiastically taken up and his domes put into production as shelters for military hardware. Nevertheless Fuller himself has made several houses out of his domes; one of the most successful was built at Yale University and made of high strength, corrugated-paper board. Fuller visualises a husband and wife buying the dome at the supermarket for a few hundred dollars; loading all the components of the house into their car; driving out to their site on the edge of the city and assembling it themselves. Like Frank Lloyd Wright, Fuller believes that there is always plenty of available land just beyond the city boundary; his 'comprehensive, anticipatory design science' has not yet taken into account the problems of town planning. In 1959, when Fuller was appointed to a teaching post at Southern Illinois University at Carbondale, he had a dome built in which to live himself. As always with a Fuller dome, the structure is very wonderful, but the plan has had to be distorted to fit the circular space, and the positioning of doors and windows is severely limited by the construction. Even so, the openings interrupt the smooth dome surface and so destroy much of its charm. Fuller's approach is the process of architectural design turned back to front.

Far left, a view showing the foundation beam in place and the hexagons stacked in the background. The completed paint tunnel can be seen in the left foreground.

Left, six lorry-mounted cranes erect the panels starting from the circumference and working towards the centre. The steel panels are only ⅛-inch thick.

Below left, some of the 321 hexagonal steel panels stacked on the site at Baton Rouge, waiting to be hoisted into place to form the world's largest dome.

Instead of studying living requirements and finding an appropriate shape and structure to house them, Fuller has shoe-horned his life into an inflexible shape. He even joked about it himself by making up a song, sung to the tune of *Home on the Range*.

Just give me a home in a great circle dome
Where the stresses and strains are at ease.
Roam home to a dome
Where Georgian and Gothic once stood;
Now chemical bonds
Alone guard our blondes
And even the plumbing looks good.

Yet when a Fuller dome is used for a building where it is the most appropriate shape, then there is no cause for humour. The simple rightness of the result is breathtaking. Such an opportunity was provided on a grand scale by the dome commissioned by the Union Tank Car Company, completed in 1958 at Baton Rouge, Louisiana. Union Tank Car needed a building in which railroad tankers could be serviced simultaneously. This would only be an economical proposition if planned on a large scale, since it had to cope with whole trainloads of cars which were to be distributed by a central

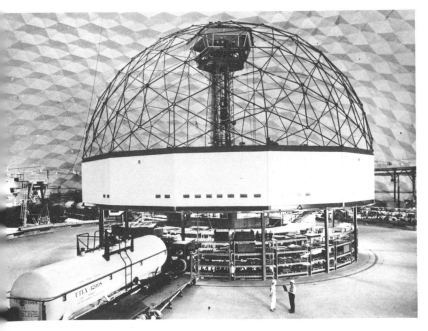

Opposite, another view of the Baton Rouge roundhouse under construction.

Inside the Baton Rouge roundhouse, left, a tanker is being shunted into its repair bay. In the centre, the open web of a dome defines the administrative area that forms the roof over the stores area.

turntable. A design to meet these requirements was worked out by Fuller's own company, Synergetics Inc. In the completed structure, the tankers enter the dome on one of three tracks, proceed to a rotating table from which they are shunted on to any one of 14 repair bays according to the repair work that has to be carried out on them. On completion of the repairs the tankers leave either directly or through the paint tunnel, if they need painting. The dome itself spans 384 feet without internal supports, and at the time of its erection was the largest dome in the world—23 times the volume of St Peter's, Rome; the height to the apex is 120 feet. It was erected by cranes working from the inside, which raised the 321 hexagonal panels, each one of folded steel braced externally with steel tubes and rods. The steel of the panels is one eighth of an inch thick, which in proportion to the span is considerably thinner than an eggshell. The weight too is only about two ounces of steel for each cubic foot enclosed, thus satisfying Fuller's basic demand for maximum performance from minimum material and resulting in a relatively low cost of $10 per square foot for the completed building.

Inside the great dome, some way off-centre, is the lace-like web of a second dome. This dome, 100 feet in diameter, surrounds the control tower and its function is purely decorative. It defines the central area, which contains the offices and restaurant at first-floor level, and the stock of replacement parts at ground-floor level. The paint tunnel is a half-cylinder of similar construction to the main dome, which it abuts like the entrance to an igloo. This paint tunnel is 200 feet long and 40 feet wide.

The Union Tank Car Company were evidently well pleased with their building, for they negotiated with Fuller for a licence to design and build steel domes in competition with those made in alloy by Kaiser Aluminium, a licensee of Fuller's, and through their subsidiary, Graver Tank and Manufacturing Company, they erected a second and similar dome in 1960 at Wood River, Illinois. Unlike the Baton Rouge dome, which was begun at the perimeter and grew from the edges towards the middle, the Wood River dome was erected by pneumatic cushion lift. A very large balloon was placed under the central panels, and as the balloon was slowly inflated, new sections were added to the edges until the dome was completed; the balloon was then removed. This system enabled all work to be done at ground level.

The form of Buckminster Fuller's domes, which allow such great spaces to be enclosed with relatively little material, may look simple

Above, the dome at Wood River, Illinois, built later than the Baton Rouge structure, but similar in function, construction and size.

Right, the completed Baton Rouge roundhouse seen from the air. The building exists to service and repair the railroad tankers of the Union Tank Car Company. The tankers enter by one of the four doors in the centre of the picture and are shunted round inside by turntable to a suitable repair bay; repaired tankers leave by the entrance on the right or through the long arm of the paint tunnel.

but are in fact very complex geometrically—so much so that their mathematics are well beyond the grasp of most structural engineers today. Both the Baton Rouge dome and the Wood River domes are made of irregular hexagonal units since regular hexagons fitted together make a flat plane, not the surface of a sphere. Fuller calls the basis of this geometry geodesic and his domes geodesic structures. The geometry is based on a three-way great-circle system, which at first sight may seem very complicated but in fact it can be seen at once that a load applied to any point will rapidly spread to many members. Thus the individual members may be small; parts of the dome may even, within reason, be omitted if required.

Fuller is an optimist. He believes that the technological advances of the last twenty-five years are waiting to be used. 'All you need now is the knowledge of what you want to do—the billion-dollars worth of anticipatorily scheduled research has been done.' Moreover, he claims that the spacecraft has made the military airplane obsolete, so the vast resources of the aircraft industry will now be looking for outlets in other directions, and find them in housing. Thus, as at other times in history, mankind's greatest brains and most advanced know-how will be at the service of the building industry.

Above, an interior view of the Wood River dome showing the tankers in their repair bays as seen from the control area in the centre.

Above right, a view inside the Wood River dome during erection. It shows the nylon curtain that makes the space under the half-built dome into a great balloon, taking the weight until the dome is completed.

Right, the Wood River dome under construction from the top down. First the central panels were jointed together, then a nylon balloon was placed under them and slowly inflated, while the builders fitted additional panels around the edges until the dome was completed. This method allowed all work to be carried out at ground level.

94

CHAPTER 6

HIGHPOINT

North Hill, London N.6

The Highpoint flats, more than any other building in England, represent the 'heroic' phase of modern architecture. This was the period during the 1930s when the issues were clear: modern architecture had logical layouts, white walls, flat roofs, and stood in opposition to the prevailing mode of building in a style copied from some period in the past. (After the war, modern architecture became that of the establishment, the situation changed and the quality dropped.) The architects of the heroic period had to surmount fantastic obstacles in order to build at all, some natural, such as working out their building and planning methods from scratch, and others artificial, created by the opposition to their ideas, which was intense and often vicious. For example, Le Corbusier's entry into the international competition for the League of Nations building at Geneva was rejected because he had drawn in printer's ink and the conditions had stipulated Chinese ink! In such an atmosphere of hostility, it would seem that only the best modern architects survived; certainly the architectural quality of the few buildings they built is astonishingly high. As was pointed out in the introduction, most modern architecture in the 1920s was German or French, but during the early 1930s Nazism in Germany and depression in France stopped the movement altogether in those countries and many of the ablest practitioners emigrated to England.

Modern architecture in England in the early 1930s was a provincial movement. The architects had talent but little experience. The situation was changed by the arrival of the Europeans—Gropius, Mendelsohn, Breuer from Germany, Lubetkin and Goldfinger from France—and quite suddenly England acquired a great deal of expertise, which the local modern architects picked up with great

The garden side of the Highpoints photographed in 1968. Highpoint 1 is on the left and Highpoint 2, built three years later, is on the right.

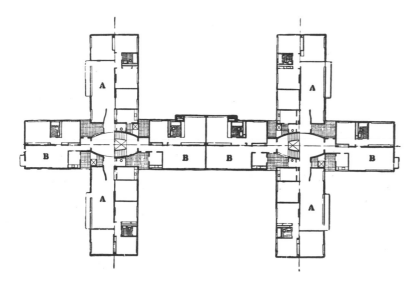

speed. Thus, for a brief period in the late 1930s, English architecture was the most important in the world, and the best built works, such as Highpoint 1, were major international events.

None of the emigrés or the locals could handle architectural forms with the verve of Lubetkin. The English moderns, very influenced by the serious, methodical Germans were stunned at his curved walls, rich colours, rough textures and occasional wilfulness. Born in Russia and educated in France, Berthold Lubetkin built a few buildings in Paris before settling in England, where he formed a partnership with young architects, one of whom, Denys Lasdun, was to become one of the most distinguished architects of the 1960s. The group, called Tecton, designed a series of houses in London and Whipsnade which were both highly inventive and pleasant to live in. The houses were very sophisticated but had a slightly light-hearted cheerfulness absent from most other modern buildings of the time, which took their revolutionary status seriously. Tecton's houses were a joy. Their Finsbury Health Centre showed that a social service could welcome the public with cheerful, generous architecture. But it was their Penguin Pool at the London Zoo that changed modern architecture in England from an esoteric movement into a popular success. The crowds that went to see the penguins waddling round the interlocking ramps saw not only a fine structure for displaying the birds, but also modern architecture, rather tongue-in-cheek, laughing at itself.

The verve and flamboyance of Lubetkin is no-where clearer than in the Penguin Pool at London Zoo, left. Here the problem is less serious than it is in housing, and the designers have obviously enjoyed making a playful penguin world and at the same time saying something serious about the nature of reinforced concrete.

The great opportunity for the Tecton group came when they were commissioned to build Highpoint 1, completed in 1935. No British building built since has been so consistently and beautifully worked out in all its details and it remains the unchallenged masterpiece of modern architecture in England. In planning, construction and equipment it was a total breakthrough at the time—so much so that the building regulations and controls were found to be irrelevant. Such a building had never been imagined by those who had drafted the codes, so Highpoint 1 was built without bureaucratic difficulties. Some of the items Highpoint 1 pioneered, such as climbing formwork, have become routine; others, such as centrally operated refrigerators, have proved blind alleys. But always there was this search for new improvements.

The site is the brow of a hill four miles north of central London. The hill is high and the top flats in Highpoint could claim to be the highest in London. The road frontage of the site was relatively narrow and there was a restrictive covenant, limiting building to the front part of the site and leaving a generous garden at the rear. The plan adopted to fit the awkward area available for building was

Above, the entrance to Highpoint 1, with a driveway for cars to drop passengers under cover at the entrance.

Opposite, Highpoint 1 in the final stages of completion in 1935. The first major building of the modern movement in England, its quality remains unequalled to this day. Before Highpoint, England was a provincial in the world architecture scene, but its completion made London the centre for a few years. 101

a double cross, with lift and staircase in the unlit area in the centre of each cross. This plan form provides excellent access, economical in the use of lifts, but its disadvantages of overshadowing and overlooking have prevented its development in subsequent buildings. The seven identical apartment floors have eight flats each, one to each arm of the double cross. The staircase walls are curved in the Tecton manner and access to the flats is cleverly contrived to give them adjacent 'front' and 'back' doors as was customary—indeed socially necessary—among the prewar professional class. The main entrance led into a spacious living room with a balcony with a wavy front—a shape Tecton had borrowed from Le Corbusier. A door the far end of the living room led into a little lobby giving access to bedrooms and bathroom. This arrangement eliminated corridors, but meant that much of the internal traffic of the flat had to go through the living room.

The top and bottom floors have different structures and plan forms from the seven identical floors in between. The roof is a promenade deck with concrete windshields, while the ground floor is a fabulous array of curving spaces. Entry is by *porte cochère*, a covered space for arrivals, curved to follow the route of the car. Inside, a great hall swings round to beyond the middle of the building to

The hallway connecting the two lifts in the ground floor of Highpoint 1.

provide a generous entrance and to give access to the two widely spaced lifts. At the far end of the block is a curved tea room looking out over the garden; in the wings of the ground floor are maids' bedrooms, so that occupants on the upper floors can have a 'living-in' maid without any loss of privacy.

Most of the flats in Highpoint 1 were let before construction was finished. Le Corbusier himself wrote a monograph in praise of the building, which he called the 'world's first vertical garden city'. But the new residents had only a year in which to appreciate their good fortune and enjoy the views before they learnt that a property company had bought the adjacent site and obtained the local authority's permission to build a sham medieval block of flats. This ghastly building, about the same size as Highpoint 1 and only a few feet away, would have cut off their views and overlooked them—in short would have ruined the site. So, after much heartsearching and negotiation, Highpoint 1 bought the adjacent site, paying considerably above market price because of their anxiety to buy.

The Tecton group then set about designing Highpoint 2 and at this point the sleepy suburbanites of Highgate awoke to fight the

Highpoint 2, completed in 1938 with the three-year-old Highpoint 1 just visible on the left. It can be seen that the gleaming white surfaces of the earlier building have already become streaked and patchy. To avoid a repetition of this, Highpoint 2 has been finished with bricks and glazed tiles.

103

threat of another Highpoint desecrating their village! A local amenities preservation society was formed specifically to stop a repetition of Highpoint 1. The local council, who had just gained powers of aesthetic control over buildings, which they did not have when Highpoint 1 was built, announced that they would not permit a building remotely resembling Highpoint 1. Lesser architects might have given up in despair, but Lubetkin's men slowly outwitted the opposition by submitting and receiving permission on a whole series of designs, mostly for semi-historical buildings, each including one feature of the block Tecton wanted to put up. For example, a design resembling the Doge's Palace in Venice gained permission for free-standing round columns on the ground floor and a scheme based on a Jacobean mansion gained permission for the shapes on the roof. Then, having gained consent for their design in this piecemeal fashion, Tecton put the parts together and built Highpoint 2, which was finished in 1938.

Opposite, a view into the penthouse built by Lubetkin for himself on top of Highpoint 2. On the inside he used rugged natural materials— quarry tiles, rough timber, hairy hides.

Below, the entrance to Highpoint 2, which like Highpoint 1, has a curved canopy for cars. Here however it is supported on casts of ancient Greek statues. These stop the little canopy from appearing too serious, but were a cause of great controversy at the time.

Inevitably, the design is not as good as it might have been and lacks the uncompromising clarity of Highpoint 1, though in both flat planning and facing materials it shows progress from the first block. But the two buildings sit together very happily. In retrospect the struggle for Highpoint 2 seems farcical, and Tecton must have been incredibly smart and the council very gullible for the building to have been built at all. Architecture, like other forms of art, has been through periods of censorship. In England, the powers of aesthetic control, given to local authorities in the mid-1930s, made the achievement of an uncompromisingly modern building very difficult. The struggle for Highpoint 2 can be compared to the court cases involving literary censorship, although it is easier perhaps to understand objections to a book such as *Lady Chatterly's Lover*, than it is to comprehend the intense hostility directed at the Highpoints.

One of the casualties of the struggle over Highpoint 2 was the size of the block. In order to be allowed to go ahead Tecton was forced to design a smaller building, which was therefore uneconomic. The clients had also had to pay through the nose for the site. To make any kind of economic sense, the clients had to charge very high rents, so the apartments in Highpoint 2 were made very gorgeous to attract rich tenants, galling as this may have been to Tecton with their commitment to the political left. The entire block contains only twelve dwellings, each a two-storey maisonette with six or seven rooms. The living rooms of the centre apartments are in part two storeys high, with magnificent glazed walls opening on to the view, and a bridge giving access to the bedrooms at upper-floor level provides the high space with its two-storey scale. But none of the rooms at the upper level opens out to form a gallery over the living room, so the double-height space does not pull the whole dwelling together as it does in Le Corbusier's buildings. Highpoint 2, like Highpoint 1, has a ground floor containing maids' rooms, and a curved canopy giving access to a generous entrance hall. However, unlike Highpoint 1, which is entered at one end, Highpoint 2 is entered through the middle of the long side, so the entrance hall simply and symmetrically gives equal access to both lifts. The handling of the space is as admirable as before, with a great curved wall covered with a map of London and the garden carried through the glass screen into the interior of the building. But the part of the entrance that caused most comment was the canopy support. Here Tecton used a cast of a female figure from the

Erechtheum, one of the temples on the Acropolis in Athens. Their fellow moderns were shocked; they expected a modern building to be completely modern and in some publications photographs showing the offending Greek figures were carefully omitted. To Lubetkin, however, they looked superbly right and that was sufficient justification. They stand too, perhaps, as a memento of the struggle and all the tongue-in-cheek historical designs that came from the Tecton office to confuse the locals.

As Highpoint 2 was in the last stages of completion, Lubetkin decided to build himself a penthouse on top. Here again his sheer delight in shapes, textures and things that simply look right shocked the doctrinaire modernists of the time, who expected an interior to be serious, functional and machine-finished. Because the building below was already in existence, the points of support, drainage, lift and so on were already determined, and it was necessary to keep the edges of the penthouse low to avoid spoiling the proportions of the whole block. Within these limitations, Lubetkin played with his living space. With his continental background, he expected a lofty living room, so he made a curved roof to give him height and yet keep the edge proportions right. The underside he painted pale blue, and under it, on the view side, he place a window 25 feet long, which could be completely slid away to open on to a terrace with a view over Kenwood House to the distant Chilterns. In the living room the 'natural' quality of materials was exaggerated: walls of pine sand-blasted to bring out the grain, shelves of travertine with unsawn edges, carpets joined together with red and blue cords passing through brass rings, and chairs covered with hairy black-and-white hide on a framework of softwood logs wedged together. There are numerous works of art: a Dutch old master, Indian sculpture and two mobiles by Alexander Calder, one a face in the fireplace whose expression changes in the chimney draught. This is a manifesto interior, a statement against the cold and the clinical; it is a place to relax in, to make a mess in. Its materials are to be touched, its chairs are to loll about in; it is not one of those places that is spoilt by being used.

With the completion of Highpoint 2, the two gardens were run together and a swimming pool built at the far end. The pool building has since been altered, and Highpoint 1 is now pale cream, which is less dramatic than the original white. Even so, after over thirty years of life the two Highpoints have altered very little.

Previous pages, left, the big room in Lubetkin's flat, which has a great curved ceiling partly to give dramatic lighting and partly to form a spacious room that did not seem to project too much above the main block at Highpoint 2.

Previous pages, right, another view of the living room. It opens up completely on its two long sides to give London's highest dwelling magnificent views over the city, Hampstead Heath and the distant Chilterns.

The cosy corner of Lubetkin's living room, right, has a rugged fireplace with a Calder mobile turning in the smoke.

CHAPTER 7

EAMES HOUSE

Chatauqua Way, Santa Monica, California

Charles and Ray Eames, a husband-and-wife team, were among the most influential designers of the 1950s. They have not only produced a series of beautifully designed objects, but are responsible for a whole new way of looking at things. Though the Eameses are international figures, they are based in Los Angeles and they have used native Californian techniques, largely by-passing the European high-art, serious-culture tradition. They combine the technical confidence of Californians with a keenness for picking up images and objects from widely different cultures. They collect peasant objects and mass-produced objects (never art objects in the conventional sense) and put them together with wit and charm to make a colourful display of unsophisticated things, selected with sophistication and made into films, cards and simply placed in their house.

In 1940, the Eameses, together with the architect Eero Saarinen, won a competition for the design of a chair sponsored by the New York Museum of Modern Art. At that time their design was too sophisticated from a technical point of view, and no manufacturer could be found to produce their chair, which demanded the bonding together of different materials. During the war, however, glueing techniques developed enormously, as did methods of forming plywood, the latter partly as a result of the Eameses' own research. In 1946 the moulded plywood chair went into production and during the next twenty years new models in various materials have been added to the range. Since 1950, parallel with their continuing work on chairs, the Eameses produced films, toys, exhibitions and displays of great quality, which, together with the chairs, produced the Eames approach—a new and happy way of looking at objects. They also altered the attitude of architects, for pre-Eames modern

The terrace at the southern end of the Eames house. The precision of the house is contrasted with exuberant natural shapes—wild vegetation and rotted old tree trunks standing up like sculpture.

Left, bric-à-brac in the Eames house. Films, natural objects and peasant objects from ancient and modern cultures placed together summarise the revolution the Eameses have brought into our way of looking at things.

Right, a photograph of the house under construction showing how it is squeezed between the hillside and the eucalyptus trees, making necessary the long concrete retaining wall to allow the building to be cut into the slope.

Below, a plan of the building as built, showing the house and studio, separated by a court, set in a straight line between the hillside and a row of eucalyptus trees.

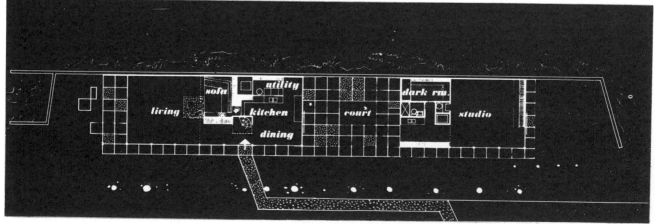

architecture was rather serious, with objects carefully placed and well related; the Eames influence led to informal interiors with light furniture, which could be moved at will, and to the replacement of serious art like painting and sculpture with the cult of collecting amusing bric-à-brac. This could either be the work of peasant cultures, such as Mexican figures, or Chinese toys or the non-high-art images of a period, as produced by the advertising industry. It is too early to assess how permanent this last change is, but it was very understandable at a time when painting had not the importance for architects it had in the 1920s, and when the advertising industry was producing images which made more impact and seemed more relevant to architects, both for the technical quality of their production and for their implications of a better life through the use of more machine-made products.

Southern California is the home of the movie industry, the air-craft industry and later the aerospace industry, and the Eameses are at home in this environment. Early modern architecture in Europe had a passionate commitment to the machine; the buildings tried to look machine-made even when they were hand-made, but their architects, for all their emotions about machines, were often ama-teurs when it came to actually using them. The Eameses, on the other hand, are not very emotional about machines; they just use them with immense competence. From the movie industry, they have taken the technique of film making and adopted it to suit their own ends. From the aircraft industry, they have studied the way alumi-nium and plastics, wood and steel are joined together and they have used this knowledge to make furniture.

The Eameses are not architects by profession, and apart from a small showroom their own house is their only built work. Yet because their minds were fresh and unencumbered with precon-ceived ideas, they were able to produce one of the most significant houses ever built and at the same time one of the most pleasant to live in. The story of the house began in 1947, when the Eameses were asked by the West Coast magazine *Arts and Architecture* to design and build a house as a 'case-study house'—one of a series of such houses commissioned by the magazine to examine the typical middle-class suburban house and to try to raise the standard by example. The Eames case-study house was to be for their own occupation and stands on a plot in Santa Monica, in the north-west part of the Los Angeles conurbation. The site was not an easy one on which to design a house, for it sloped steeply away from the sea,

Opposite, top, a general view across the meadow-like garden showing the house on the left and the studio on the right. The steel frame, the windows and all other elements of the building are stand-ard items from catalogues. The result is not architecture in the conventional sense, consistent to the smallest detail, but an attractive collection of ready-mades, like a collage.

Opposite, bottom, the house seen from the studio, looking across the brick-paved court. The retaining wall and hillside are on the right. 115

and was well wooded with eucalyptus trees. The first published design shows a large living area, raised above the ground to accommodate the slope and to take advantage of the views over the Pacific. The structure consisted of four steel posts and, since the distance between them was considerable, the steel structure is predominant and is expressed like a bridge; it is in fact a development of an idea for a steel house sketched by Mies van der Rohe twenty years earlier. At right angles to this house in the air, a studio was to have been built, cut into the hillside so as to be two-storeys high on the entrance side, and one-storey high at the back.

This design was abandoned, however, before the house was built. In the final scheme, the studio remained where it was, and the house was swung round to become a continuation of it, separated by a patio, so the house too is cut into the hillside—a fundamental change from a bridge-like structure held up in the air to an earth-hugging house cut deep into the hillside. The house has now become a two-storey building with the living area on the ground floor. This sacrifices the fine distant views, but in compensation, the living room is taken up through two floors opening out on to a covered terrace. So there are now generous internal views to make up for the distant ones that have been lost. All these changes are in sympathy with the fundamental alteration into a more introverted house. The new siting of the house in the bank behind the line of 90-foot eucalyptus trees enabled the trees to be preserved and to shelter the house from the sun, and the flat part of the site could revert to meadow—a process encouraged by cultivating only plants that were native to the site.

In 1949 the house was built. First a strong reinforced concrete retaining wall, 200 feet long, to hold back the hill and give a flat base for the house, the studio, the patio and the terrace. Then a light structure was built for the house itself, made of standard elements out of catalogues, which resulted in a house that was cheaper than average, with that non-arty quality possessed by assemblies of ready-mades, collections of other peoples' work stuck together like a collage. And because local industry offered a generous array of products, the Eameses were able to select what they needed, so that the finished building on its site is a unique and magical place. It represents a novel way of building houses: not the one-off handicraft way, for in a technically advanced society such houses can only be for the rich. (In any case, such a method seems irrelevant at a time when the best products are machine-made.) Nor is it a

116

A view of the timber walkway linking the house and studio.

Another view of the timber walkway alongside the house. The diagonal braces take the wind load and enable the construction of the house to be very light. It is this lightness that gives the house its charm and slightly unreal quality.

standardised dwelling produced by the promoters of industrialised building systems, for they leave us no freedom of choice and our needs and tastes are not all identical. The Eames house shows that out of an array of mass-produced, machine-made components we can select those we need and build an individual building. Thus we reap the benefits of mass-production and of technologically sophisticated components yct arc frcc to assemble them in our own way. It is like a giant Meccano set.

The Eames house and studio have a skeleton of steel, with 4 inch by 4 inch steel columns regularly spaced at intervals of 7 feet 4 inches along the long sides. Spanning between these two rows of columns, 20 feet apart, are 12-inch deep open truss joists. Wherever the external skin is placed across the building between two columns the 12-inch joist is omitted and the roof is supported on the mullions. As a result of this simple device, the glass on all sides can be taken right up to the roof, not up to the underside of the beam. So the roof shows an edge only a few inches thick all round and this makes the whole house look paper thin. The building and its steel frame not only are light and elegant, but also appear so. This aspect of the design is further emphasised by hiding the heavy edge beam to the upper floor and by making the steel columns too thin to take any but vertical loads and by taking wind loads on clearly expressed diagonal braces.

The steel columns and the open joists spanning them are all clearly

Left, a view looking into the front door of the Eames house showing the plywood and steel spiral staircase.

The landscape is reflected in the glass as we look into the living room, right, along the passage to the entrance door. The living room is the full height of the house and the front of the gallery makes a thick white band above head height.

Below, the inside of the studio, which, like the living room, is a two-storey-high space with a gallery. All the elements—staircase, ceiling, windows—show the same light touch with off-the-peg, machine-made items.

exposed, as is the industrial steel decking that spans between the joists to form the upper floor and the roof. The skin stretched between the columns is glazed or solid as necessary; the design can accommodate either in any position and indeed allows for them to change at a later date. The solid panels are steel industrial sheeting, plastered to give a smooth finish; the glazing is standard industrial sash, the window units selected are subdivided into small panes so that the window does not disappear but is seen as part of the membrane enclosing the space. This is further reinforced in places by glazing with wired glass, so that the glass itself becomes a visible part of the enclosure. The nature of the house is further emphasised by colour: the steel, both structural frames and window frames, are painted dark grey, and some of the infill panels in light primary colours.

When handed over, many modern buildings are completely finished; little alteration is expected and the owners have only to maintain them in their original condition. But the Eameses were building for themselves, and they knew that they would continually change the house as they designed new chairs, collected new objects or threw out old ones. Therefore the house was never designed as a finished article but as a place capable of change. The design as a

118

Above, *a view of the spiral staircase just inside the front door; beyond the cupboard is the high living room with the terrace beyond.*

whole is not symmetrical or formal in any sense; the number of columns along the sides is not of crucial design importance as it is in, say, a Greek temple. In fact, the building could have been built longer or shorter without detracting from the design. Moreover the windows are placed wherever convenient without relation to any preconceived idea of architectural order. This represents a fundamentally different view of architecture from the Renaissance belief that a design was perfect only when nothing could be added or taken away without spoiling it. The Eames approach is sometimes called 'additive architecture', because it is an assembly of pieces added together, not an unalterable harmonious whole. Inside the house there is the same lack of permanence. Photographs taken in 1949 show the living room as elegant, sparsely furnished, with bare white walls; ten years later the room had become a museum of collected items, overflowing everywhere. The pristine look had gone, replaced by one that was cosy and highly decorated. The house can accept the changes. It was designed to.

The arrangement of the various rooms within the house is sensible, and much has been sacrificed to make the living room and the studio a generous size and the full height of the building. The result is the same wonderful sense of spaciousness as the similar arrangement of its contemporary, Le Corbusier's Unité d'Habitation at Marseille (described in Chapter 1). In the house the upper floor covers about half the area and is reached by an elegant spiral staircase without a handrail—this is an adults only house! The two bedrooms are on

Opposite, the living room photographed twelve years after completion. Originally the room was white and rather severe, but it has acquired a new character as it has become filled with objects and furniture over the years.

121

this upper floor, and as well as normal windows opening on the outside, they have sliding panels so that they can be opened to become balconies looking down into the big living room; underneath these bedrooms is a low annex to the living room forming a cosy corner for more intimate occasions. The living room, 24 feet by 20 feet by 17 feet high, seems even larger than it is because the ceiling continues into the bedrooms and out over the terrace. The house must be one of the finest ever built in which to enjoy a sunny climate, with its easy relationship of high inside room to paved terrace with sheltering retaining wall and trees, a roof extending 7 feet 6 inches beyond the glass line to cut out the high summer sun and windows on three sides to catch the breezes. The terrace is paved with brick divided into square panels as an extension of the same geometry of the house's structure; and here there are often new designs of Eames chairs, which they are trying out themselves and a cluster of tree trunks set up like sculpture.

A house designed for the film director Billy Wilder by Charles and Ray Eames after completing their own house. This design takes the ideas of the Eames house a stage further; not only is the steel frame more light and elegant than ever, but the plan is allowed to wander informally.

After completing the house, the Eameses started making films and built no more. And although the influence of the Eames way of looking at objects has been taken up by designers all over the world, the house as a building has had little direct influence, and the many possibilities it opens up for domestic architecture are still largely unexplored. Many of the later case-study houses commissioned by *Arts and Architecture* are also framed in steel, but they have reverted to a heavier, more formal architecture, as opposed to the delicate, sophisticated informality of the Eames house. The Eameses themselves reinforced their message with a design for a house for the film director Billy Wilder, prepared shortly after they moved into their own house, but it was never constructed. The Billy Wilder house emphasises, even more than their own house, the lightness of steel construction and an informal, almost rambling disposition of rooms and terraces. Other architects, under the influence of Mies van der Rohe, admired steel structure for the simplicity of their members and the regular layout it seemed to imply. But the Eameses made the layout wander to suit their requirements and made their beams not of simple I-sections but of built-up trusses so that individual steel members are very small and the whole effect is so light that it appears almost unbuildable.

Architects tend to be rather serious about their work. Perhaps the greatest lesson of the Eames house is that it showed that it was possible to design a serious building that is relaxing to use and to decorate it in a way that amuses as well as pleases.

CHAPTER 8

OFFICE BUILDING FOR
THE UPJOHN COMPANY

Portage Road, Kalamazoo, Michigan

In the past, the buildings of commerce have been situated at the heart of things, in the market place. For commerce to flourish, personal contact has to be made with many people and it was to the market that everybody came. With the development of railways, city centres became the most accessible places, because they were near the great termini and well served by public transport. So in the railway age great business centres such as downtown Manhattan and the Chicago Loop were built. These were densely built, high building next to high building, so that as many people as possible might work within easy visiting distance of one another. Today, however, we are entering an age when the motor car is superseding public transport as the preferred method of travelling, while the telephone and other forms of communication are reducing the need for personal contact. This means that while the telephone reaches everywhere the motorist finds the centres of great cities extremely inconvenient, since the roads are crowded and there can never be enough parking space. Moreover, as more and more people live in the suburbs, and the daily journey to work becomes more unpleasant year by year, there is no reason why offices should not follow their staff into the suburbs. In Europe, shortage of land and strict planning controls have sharply restricted the growth of building in the country-side or on the outer fringe of cities. In the United States, on the other hand—particularly in the Midwest and on the West Coast—the amount of land seems limitless and activities of all kinds tend to decentralise and spread themselves thinly over vast tracts of land. Thus the city in the traditional sense has ceased to exist. This sprawl development has taken place at the same time as the further development of the old railway-age centres. Take for example the

Seagram building in Manhattan, which is solving precisely the same office problems as the Upjohn building on the Michigan prairie. It is the difference in location that makes these two buildings so dissimilar.

The architects responsible for the Upjohn building were Skidmore, Owings and Merrill, who, with the Architects Department of the Greater London Council, are the largest architectural offices in the world. The fact that both have designed one of the buildings included in this book should indicate that a large, rather impersonal organisation is just as capable of producing fine architecture as a small firm, though it will probably be more anonymous and·less likely to be marked by irrationalities, either good or bad. Skidmore, Owings and Merrill have served American business competently, if not always brilliantly, since the days of the Depression. They have offices in New York, Chicago, San Francisco and Portland, and in 1951 they completed Lever House on New York's Park Avenue. This glass-covered building had an aura of the fabulous to those living in the rather dreary postwar world. It was the building of the moment and a smash hit; its glassy curtain wall was copied around the world, and its architects were rewarded with many more commissions from American Big Business. During the early 1950s the firm built up an international reputation with its glassy, elegant skyscrapers in the centres of cities, for Chase Manhattan, Union Carbide and Pepsi-Cola in New York City, for Crown Zellerbach in San Francisco, for Inland Steel in Chicago. Since the late 1950s, however, much of their output has been equally elegant buildings in the country for similar clients—for Connecticut General near Hartford, for United Air Lines in Illinios, for Reynolds Aluminium in Virginia, and in England, for Heinz at Hillingdon in Middlesex and Boots near Nottingham. These latter buildings are the architectural successors to the Palladian mansions such as Chatsworth or Blenheim belonging to 18th-century English aristocrats, where a free-standing, elegant building is surrounded by countryside, made more natural than nature by the landscape architect to contrast with the geometric, obviously man-made building.

One country office building designed by the Chicago office of Skidmore, Owings and Merrill is the headquarters building of the Upjohn Company, a pharmaceutical manufacturing firm. This building, near Kalamazoo, a town on the highway from Detroit to Chicago, was finished in 1961 and stands on a hundred acre site; it is the international headquarters of the company and it houses

Opposite, an aerial view showing the building and part of its park. With their precise, four-square buildings set in great parks with artificial lakes and romantic planting, the American out-of-town office building is the architectural equivalent of the 18th-century Palladian mansion set in a man-made landscape.

Below, a plan of the building. Note the courtyards that give an outlook to the rooms in the middle of the 432-foot-square building.

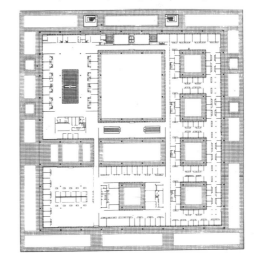

their central office management, sales, legal and finance departments.

The architects investigated many possible building forms, but eventually decided on a spreading, low building because it settled down well on the prairie site. It was also felt that, by having all offices on one floor, staff from the different departments would mingle with ease. The building has two floors: the lower level contains all the service rooms—lavatories, canteen, mechanical equipment and storage—and the upper level is devoted to offices. The upper level is pierced by nine landscaped courtyards, so that although the building is 432 feet square every office has a window with a pleasant outlook. The way in, both for those driving into the building and for those walking from the parking lot, is on the lower level. The entrance is elegant but has a rather subterranean feeling with a low textured ceiling and an underground garden—not a garden in the conventional sense with growing plants but a composition of rocks and raked sand inspired by an old Japanese sand garden near Kyoto. The sandy, beige tones and incandescent lighting intensify the underground atmosphere; but once inside the space opens out to a generous lobby with escalators leading up to the office floor above. This lobby is lit and decorated by a courtyard 144 feet square containing a pool and a row of trees. This large courtyard, unlike the other, smaller ones, is taken down through both floors of the building and on the lower floor, rooms where activities are carried out that gain from natural light are placed around it. Since the upper floor is where the staff have their offices and do their work, this floor is made to appear important on the outside, while the lower floor, housing service rooms that do not require natural light, is played down architecturally. From the outside the lower floor is seen as a mere plinth for the offices.

Like other modern office buildings, the Upjohn headquarters are designed to have a flexible interior layout. The aim is to achieve a design that will inhibit present and future office requirements to the least extent, so that the building does not become inconvenient or out of date as a result of the changing needs of the Upjohn Company. To achieve this flexibility office buildings are supported on columns and not on walls. These columns are placed as far apart as is possible because, when laying out offices, columns are a nuisance since they cannot be moved and so restrict the placing of partitions and furniture. In the Upjohn building the columns are 48 feet apart, and are mostly outside the building, so that they can never be in the

126

Right, a night shot showing newly-planted trees silhouetted against brightly lit offices.

Below right, a view of the site, which was flat farmland until the landscape architects had the lakes dug, the grass sown and the trees planted to give an effect of instant permanence—an idea reinforced by the chunky stone walls round the base of the building.

Below, part of the roof structure of a three-dimensional steel structure of pyramids with their apexes connected, which enables long spans to be constructed economically.

way. The interior of the building is subdivided into rooms by partitions and, because the roof is supported by the columns, these partitions serve no structural purpose and are easily demountable. They can therefore be moved whenever an area of the building is reorganised. Even so, because of the complexity of bringing air, heat, light, electrical and telephone outlets to each and every room, these partitions can only be set up in certain positions. This partitioning grid varies with the type of office a particular building is likely to need, and the choice is a serious matter since the closer the lines of the grid the more expensive the building. In the Upjohn building, the grid is 6 feet. This means that every 6-foot square contains all the mechanical services and each length of partition and each window is 6 feet wide. Thus the dimensions of every room and the distance between the columns must always be a multiple of 6 foot and storage walls, filing cabinets and so on are all made to conform to the same measurement. Internally, the building is given its character by the continuous expression of the grid, so that no matter how much future occupants move their partitions and change the spaces within their building, the essential feel of the architecture is unchanged, because the 6-foot square ceiling panels and the glazing mullions 6 feet apart will remain as long as the building lasts and impose a discipline on all arrangements and rearrangements inside. This exemplifies one of the ways in which architects are trying to tackle the difficult, characteristically 20th-century problem of making satisfying architecture when the use of a building is continually changing, and it may soon be required to cater for activities that could not even be guessed at at the time of construction. The consideration of this problem is not only necessary from a practical point of view, but represents a fundamental architectural rethink to satisfy the needs of the time.

The Upjohn building is entirely air-conditioned, partly so that it is clean and comfortable to work in, and partly so that rooms can, where necessary, be placed away from windows and still be well ventilated. In addition, the broad overhang of the roof, as well as expressing the structure and symbolising shelter, keeps out the heat of the summer sun when it is high in the sky yet does not impede the warming, more oblique rays of the sun in winter. This saves fuel since the air-conditioning system does not have to work so hard to keep the building cool in summer and the heating plant need not generate so much heat on sunny winter days. The overhang also cuts out some of the glare of the bright prairie sky, which would

Above, a detail of the elevation including one of the cruciform columns that stand outside the building and part of the glazed wall with uprights 6 feet apart, so that partitions can be placed at those points.

All the offices are on one floor, and the lower level, partly sunk into the ground, contains all the service rooms. In the view, opposite top, this differentiation can be seen externally: the office floor is fully glazed under its elegant roof canopy while the unglazed lower floor is a mere plinth for the office floor to stand on.

Opposite below, a view showing how the ground slopes downwards to allow for an entrance for cars at the lower level.

otherwise cause discomfort to people working on the perimeter of the building.

The lower floor, largely buried in the ground, is constructed of reinforced concrete; the upper floor, light, elegant and with all glass walls on all sides, is framed in steel—a choice of structural materials that appropriately emphasises the different character and different functions of the two floors. The steel roof is supported by steel columns set 48 feet apart in both directions. The roof structure spans in both directions and this fact is logically and clearly revealed by giving the steel columns the shape of a Greek cross on plan. (The cost of a steel structure is built up partly from materials and partly from labour, and these two variables give a considerable range of solutions that are possible economically. And, since it is a tenet of modern architects that structure should be clear and logical, the same range is probably also possible architecturally.) In the Upjohn building the roof is a space deck—a system of construction in which the members are placed three dimensionally. Since this is a very

Left, the typing area with an outlook on to the courtyard. The pyramids of the space-frame roof are clearly demonstrated by the ceiling panels, which divide the plan into 6-foot squares. Lights are at the top of the ceiling pyramids, which act as baffles against glare.

Right, two of the private offices, here 12 feet by 18 feet. Glass at high level in the partitions and glazed doors emphasise the feeling of openness.

light form of construction it has a low weight of steel but a large number of joints, which means high labour costs—unlike, for example, Crown Hall, a simple steel building with large expensive steel members but few joints, so cutting labour costs. When designing a steel structure, an engineer aims to have (among other things) as much as possible fabricated in the workshop and to keep to a minimum the work on the site, since this is expensive and difficult to supervise. For the Upjohn building, areas of roof 12 foot by 66 foot by 3 foot deep were made 160 miles away in Detroit and transported to the site where they were bolted together to make a continuous deck.

Opposite, the large courtyard, which extends through two floors to provide an outlook for the entrance and reception area at the lower level. The other eight courtyards do not penetrate the lower storey.

A typical small courtyard. Unlike the informal park outside, the courtyard gardens are very formal and architectural.

Steel has the most favourable strength to volume ratio of all normal building materials, but it rapidly loses its strength if the temperature rises above normal. So in all major buildings steel must be protected from heat in the event of fire. This, so far unsolved, technical problem is perhaps the main reason for the building industry's difficulty in becoming industrialised; it also raises architectural problems, for how can a designer express the structure of his building if he has to cover it up? In the Upjohn building the roof is protected by pyramid-shaped plaster ceiling coffers, which fit into the underside of the 6-foot square pyramids of the space deck. At the apex of each of these plaster pyramids are four lights with baffles so that illumination is directed downwards and the source of light is not normally seen. This arrangement gives enough direct light for objects to have shadow and be clearly seen, yet the lighting is soft and free from glare. Where the edge of the roof shows externally the architects have made it express the character of the structure as clearly as a fire-resisting covering will permit. This covering—a plaster spray, which also acts as thermal insulation—is itself covered with eighth of an inch thick panels of aluminium with a porcelainised finish, shaped into triangular panels to help to explain the nature of the structure that they protect.

The site was once a flat field, but bulldozers and graders have transformed it into a delightful stretch of countryside with hills and valleys, groves of trees and lakes with swans on them. This setting, almost too idyllic to be true, provides a wonderful outlook for the offices as well as convincing proof of the advantage of building outside the city. The entire site is ringed with four rows of trees to exclude all sight of the world beyond, so that it would not matter if the area was engulfed by suburban sprawl. In contrast, the seven small courts inside the building have a concrete roof as a base. They are therefore not landscaped 'naturally' like the planting around the building, but are formally laid out as part of the architecture of the building.

Not surprisingly most people travel by car to a building in such a place. The vast car park provided is sited beyond the avenue of trees that rings the site, so that cars do not mar the view from the offices. The walk from car park to entrance is direct, flanked by formal lakes containing islands and trees that contrast with the meandering, informal quality of most of the landscaping—a route that aptly expresses the purposeful, usually hurried journey from car to entrance.

The long, narrow courtyard with fountains in the centre of the Upjohn building.

CHAPTER 9

SIEDLUNG HALEN

Kirchindach, near Berne, Switzerland

The problem of housing is fascinating because it does not really seem capable of solution. Many brave architects have struggled with it and been found wanting. The requirements are always conflicting: we want views out through generous windows but not people looking in; we want our own patch of garden but not to be too far out of town; we want to live in a private castle and yet be part of a community; we want to bring our car to the front door, but our children to be safe from traffic hazards; we want our home to be a beautiful place, yet one in which the kids can muck about; we want it well built and insulated against outside cold and noise, but we are rarely able to put down the cash.

In addition to all these genuine difficulties, housing has the disadvantage of coming at the 'wrong' end of the social scale. So much so, that it would not be too much of an exaggeration to say that in London, for example, postwar housing developments become duller to look at and less satisfactory to live in as they ascend the financial ladder. At one end of the scale there are public authority estates for their tenants, which are seriously and considerately designed but usually too committee-ridden to be very enjoyable; at the other end, the rich usually value seclusion and live in one-off houses shut away from their neighbours; and in the middle, the jerry-builder builds as shoddily as the councils and mortgage companies will allow, with an almost total absence of playgrounds or other communal amenities—in other words, there is nowhere to go but 'out'.

In Switzerland seven architects, working under the group name Atelier 5, were involved in the purchase of an area of woodland about four kilometres from Berne. They determined to tackle the

The planting is so intense, and the attempts to give the dwellers privacy is so successful, that Seidlung Halen is difficult to photograph. However, there is no privacy from the air, and this aerial view reveals the tightly packed residential complex set in woodland.

housing problem for themselves and like-minded friends, and after the inevitable problems of capitalising such a venture they were successful. In 1960 the occupants moved in. The site was ideal: it was near the Wohlensee in beautiful country; it was thickly wooded; it sloped southwards to the water and a great arched bridge. The trees are so thick that the only view is that facing downhill towards the snow-capped peaks of the Alps, spread across the landscape in a magnificent panorama. The site is also totally isolated; no other buildings or signs of habitation can be seen from it. But having found the perfect location, the question was, how to build? The garden-city enthusiasts would have divided the land into plots and built cottages, but this would have sacrificed the woodland and made the site like any other featureless suburb. Le Corbusier would have built one Unité d'Habitation; this would have preserved the site, but why drive three miles out of the city in order to raise children in a block of flats?

The Atelier 5 solution is so logical and direct that, like many good designs, it has an air of inevitability about it. First, they cleared an area in the middle of the site for building, leaving the thick woodland all around as a place in which to play and as insulation from the outside world. In the clearing they placed two terraces of houses. Each house was made very deep and narrow, so that as many as reasonable could be included without making the terraces too long. Because the terraces run along the contours, one is higher than the other; thus the upper terrace looks over the roof of the lower, and each house has a view south to the mountains. Every house has its own walled garden, so that as well as the woodland around, which is shared by all, each family has its own private outdoor space. Indeed, private is a key word in describing the whole development. The architects have gone to fantastic lengths to ensure privacy. By clever planning, they have made it almost impossible for passers-by to look into the houses or gardens; windows, balcony fronts and roofs are all carefully detailed to prevent any invasion of one's neighbours' privacy. In this casbah there are whole walls of glass and everyone can sit out in the sun, but completely secluded. The skill and cunning with which this privacy has been achieved is fantastic. A curious visitor to Halen trying to see what the houses are like or to peep into the walled gardens will be frustrated; every time he thinks he has found a vantage point he will find some device to thwart him. When he goes into a house he will be amazed at how that which has seemed so closed now seems so open. But when

Opposite, summer and winter views of the central walkway seen from the east. To the right is a terrace of type 380 houses, with their gardens extending across the roofs of the little studio dwellings. Alternate houses in the type 380 terrace are given a different top-floor plan, so the elevation pops up and down to accommodate this. In the centre can be seen the flue that serves the central-heating boiler and marks the little square in the centre of the development.

he leaves, he will have seen only one house; its neighbours remain almost as unknown as before. Not surprisingly, then, Halen is almost impossible to photograph meaningfully except from the air and the photographs in this chapter were all taken soon after completion, before the luxuriant vegetation had all but submerged the scheme.

The Halen development provides 79 dwellings; 33 of these are large and called type 12 houses, 41 are small and are called type 380 houses. All houses of each type have private gardens. In addition to these family houses there are five studios. One of the aims of the Halen development is to combine the advantages of owner-occupation with the communal amenities usually found only in developments of rented housing. So, although each house is owned by its occupant (who is responsible for its maintenance and may resell on the free market), the Siedlung Halen, a registered commercial company, provides generous amenities: a swimming pool, a café, a shop, garage space and a petrol service station. The company also imposes certain rules on the occupants and is responsible for the general administration of the estate.

Both the type 12 and type 380 houses are about 48 feet from front 140 to back; the type 380 is 12 feet 6 inches wide and has the staircase

The central town square with a café and shop. Although primarily a pedestrian development with a car park and garage at the entrance, it is nevertheless possible to bring in the occasional vehicle when necessary—for example, in an emergency or to service the shop.

at right angles to the party walls. However, the type 12 is some 4 feet wider and this extra width not only makes the interior spaces more generous but enables the staircase to be placed parallel to the party walls. This allows greater freedom in planning the interior, which is no longer split into two by the staircase. Because of the slope of the site, all houses are two storeys high on the entrance side and three storeys high on the garden side; the entrance is on the living floor with bedrooms above and below.

The type 380 house is entered from a covered way, which runs along the front of the terrace so that residents can move about the site or go to their cars under shelter. The front door leads into a tiny courtyard, one side of which is roofed to form a covered access to the house itself. Inside the house there is a kitchen in the front, while the staircase, placed across the house, divides off the back half of the entrance floor into the dining/living room, with a wide balcony at the back looking southwards to the Alps and a little staircase leading down to the back garden on the floor below. The party walls each side of the house extend beyond the face of the building to prevent the living room from overlooking the neighbouring gardens. Below the living room is a space, which can be turned to whatever use the occupants may wish: it can stay as one big room and be used

The café at dusk. Here the residents can meet and talk and entertain their friends. Note the planting on the canopy. All the Halen roofs are planted, for the sloping site means that most of them are overlooked by bedroom windows. A few years after completion much of this planting had spilled over the roof like a hanging garden.

141

Left, the entrance hall of a type 12 house. The far door is the street door, and leads into a covered way down the side of a tiny, private front garden to the door of the house itself.

Right, a typical living room with balcony beyond. Inside the balcony, steps lead down to the garden. The side walls of the room continue out to the face of the balcony to reduce overlooking from one house to the neighbour's garden below.

as a study, workshop, bedroom or garden room, or it can be sub-divided to form two children's bedrooms, long and narrow like those in Le Corbusier's Marseille building. These rooms on the lowest floor open on to the garden, which is walled to give it privacy. Part of the garden may extend on to the roof of other buildings, but it is provided with enough earth for planting, The end of the garden is like a balcony, enclosed by high side walls and a handrail-height wall at the end to open the garden up to the view to the south. Part of the far part of the garden is roofed to prevent it from being overlooked by the neighbour's living room, and, incidentally, forming a pleasant place in which to sit outside.

Upstairs from the living room is a floor with three bedrooms. The north-facing bedroom has a small window and a generous roof light so that it shall not seem too sunless. The bedrooms facing south are fully glazed, but outside the windows is a great concrete frame with a horizontal slab above roof level to keep out the high summer sun and a similar slab at floor level to prevent people in the bedrooms from overlooking their neighbours' garden. In an alternative design for the type 380 houses, there is less enclosed space on the top floor but a balcony instead. And by mixing houses of the different kinds in the same terrace, the architects have made the elevations of their long terraces come to life; in the model made before construction, the houses in each terrace were identical. Photographs of this model show that this would have been a dreary arrangement; as built, the sunshades over the bedrooms pop up like giant eyebrows.

The type 12 house is similar in general arrangement to the type 380, but, as pointed out earlier, is more generous in its dimensions and has a second bathroom. Entry into type 12 is through a two-storey high entrance hall with staircase, and this gives a visitor an impression of greater luxury than the rather narrow entrance corridor of the type 380. Like the type 380, the type 12 is also built with a solarium top floor—a splendid private walled garden in the sky.

There are many minor variations to the design of the house types. Some type 12s are linked to ateliers, which double their size; at the other extreme there are studios with a bed space on the gallery. Generally speaking, in fact, Halen can provide for most family sizes and requirements.

Cars approach Halen from the west. There is an underground car park for residents' cars hollowed out of the ground under the

Above, a view of a type 12 house with a sun terrace on the top floor, surrounded by high walls to the north, east and west to give shelter and privacy. The complicated shapes of the concrete balustrades are all designed to reduce overlooking.

Opposite, the interior of a studio, another type of house design provided at Halen.

145

garden of one of the terraces of type 12, while visitors park in an open space to the west. Beyond the car park the entire development is reserved for pedestrians, and is therefore quiet and safe for children, although when necessary a vehicle can be driven across the site— say, a van to provision the shop or an ambulance in an emergency. In the centre of Halen is the town square, including a café with tables outside under the trees, a provision store and the boiler house with a chimney. This chimney has a rather formal air, like the tower of some Italian municipal building, which is strangely at odds with the relaxed character of everything else at Halen.

Atelier 5, in all their work, are deeply committed to Le Corbusier, and it is this bond of a common admiration that has enabled them to function as a coherent group when so many other architectural teams have disintegrated. A parallel on a larger scale would be the Chicago office of Skidmore, Owings and Merrill, which, at its most creative periods, has been carried along by the architects' common admiration of Mies van der Rohe. Some details at Halen, such as the concrete balcony fronts with square holes, the grass on the roof, the long thin bedrooms, come direct from postwar Le Corbusier buildings; the general layout is also based on one of his projects. Even so, there is a charm about the place and an easy, unforced

confidence about the buildings for which Atelier 5 is alone responsible; such qualities are usually only found in vernacular buildings, and it is one of the delights of Halen that it does not shout 'look at me, I am the brave new world', like so many other modern buildings.

The construction is of concrete. Elements that are frequently repeated, such as roofs and staircases, are precast; other parts of the structure are of poured-in-place concrete, with the marks of the formwork left visible, though it is much more precisely made than on a late Le Corbusier building, so its imprint is much less striking. Non-structural walls are made of brick, cement rendered externally and painted white. The problem of sound insulation between dwellings has been considered as important as the provision of privacy and paid similar attention. Each house is structurally separate from its neighbour and the walls between houses are built up of two skins with an air space between. Part of this air space is filled with polystyrene to give the best acoustic value. All the roofs are flat with a kerb round the edge to form a tray of earth with grass on it; the technical advantages are that the roof provides insulation to keep top rooms warm and minimises thermal movement in the concrete but the principal merit is visual. The roofs of the lower building form the foreground to the view from the upper ones; most flat roofs are unattractive, but at Halen they form a carpet of grass.

Heating is centralised from the central boiler house and services generally are more communally organised than in most estates. Electricity, for example, is distributed without individual meters in the houses. Halen is not beyond criticism. Are we all so obsessive about our privacy? Where do the extroverts live? Is a shop with a captive population of 70 families and no competition viable commercially? And on the social level, the price of 130,000–150,000 Swiss francs per house has made it an upper-middle-class ghetto, whereas sociologists tell us that we need a mixture of social groups to make a community. In economic terms, too, it is unfortunate that much of the cost has been absorbed by expensive items such as the underground garage and the cutting of buildings into the hillside, so the cash available for the individual houses provides only modest standards of space and amenity. Moreover, the concrete structure is heavy and inflexible, incapable of alteration. Thus any major change in the way we live or the equipment we use could render it obsolete. Even so, we must remember that here we are dealing with housing, that most insoluble of problems, and that in spite of its faults Halen provides a truly wonderful place in which to live.

Another aerial view of the Seidlung Halen in its beautiful setting near the Wohlensee.

CHAPTER 10

HOUSING AT
ROEHAMPTON, LONDON

Alton West Estate, Roehampton Lane, London

A feature of public-authority housing is that it is usually built with a modest budget on slum-clearance sites. So, however well-designed the individual buildings may be, the site and surroundings are usually dreary and landscaping is minimal. The architecture at Roehampton is no better than that of some other estates in London; it is the quality of the site that makes it so sensational.

The London County Council started building dwellings in the late 19th century and today claims to be the largest housing authority in the world. Architecturally, its high points occurred in the 1890s and the 1950s; during the first of these periods, the idealistic socialism of the followers of Morris and the Arts and Crafts Movement produced a crop of architects who designed in a relaxed, rather peasant-like way. The Millbank Estate behind the Tate Gallery is a good example. This was followed by a period when housing seemed to be regarded as a straight arithmetical problem of accommodating as many families as possible and the large depressing neo-Georgian blocks of the 1930s are our legacy. Most of the housing was designed by the council's own architectural staff and in the 1950s the quality of their work was again high; this high standard was fostered by a policy of allowing and indeed encouraging groups of young architects only a few years out of architectural school to make design decisions. In the housing division of the Architects Department there are about twenty groups working under the senior architects, and it is at group level that architectural decisions are made. This staffing system is the opposite of the old method whereby a top architect sketched his design and left it to his juniors to 'draw up'. At County Hall the sketches are produced by the group while the senior architects are involved in policy decisions

An aerial view of the Alton West Estate with Richmond Park to the right. Here the LCC aimed for a mixed development with high and low buildings, point blocks, slab blocks, terraced houses and schools in one great complex with the population of a country town.

150

not in day-to-day architectural ones. Such groups, lacking strong design leadership from their superiors, can easily dissipate their energies in internal squabbles and find themselves unable to pull in a common direction. But other groups may find a common direction and become very productive; in the case of the Roehampton group the common inspiration came from Le Corbusier. The members of the team had seen the Unité d'Habitation at Marseille and were convinced that it represented the best yet in medium-density housing. Thus on the basis of their knowledge and admiration of Le Corbusier these young men formed themselves into a team and designed and built on a scale larger than anything their master had ever constructed. It was they who realised Le Corbusier's vision of *La Ville Radieuse*, the city of towers standing in parkland; they also had the modesty and sense to know their limitations. Thus while in Le Corbusier's buildings we find flamboyance and the wild and wilful shaping of concrete, at Roehampton we find order and logic in control.

The site at Roehampton was an area about 10 miles south-west of central London where wealthy Victorians had built very large suburban villas. These houses had gardens on the scale of country estates, which were big enough to have been landscaped like parkland and old enough for the trees planted to have matured. Two of the houses are distinguished architecturally and have been retained—Downshire House and Mount Clare, the latter designed by the notable architect Henry Holland. Social changes brought an end to suburban life on this scale, and after the war the London County Council acquired 130 acres of this area. They developed the eastern half as the Alton East Estate in 1952-54, and the western half, largely completed by the end of 1958, is officially known as the Alton West Estate, but is more usually referred to as Roehampton Estate.

To the LCC's Architects Department, brought up on slum-clearance and bomb-damaged sites, the Roehampton landscape was like a dream come true: magnificent trees, sweeping lawns, a little classical temple and a mile long frontage to the south on to Richmond Park, from where herds of deer roam up to the edge of the site. With infinite care and respect they set about inserting into this landscape a development the size of a country town: 1875 dwellings for 6500 persons, a shopping centre, schools, shops, library and all other amenities. (By chance, many of the occupants are families displaced by highway improvement schemes and are therefore more mixed socially than is usual in public-authority housing.) The long

Point blocks tower above low-rise dwellings and the single-storey old people's houses.

frontage on to the park, while obviously a great attraction, caused the designers many worries, for the amenities of Richmond Park were to be jealously guarded. A 100-foot height limit was imposed on all the buildings, and the architects' first scheme, designed to give as many flats as possible views southward over the park, was rejected by the Ministries of both Housing and Works on the grounds that it presented a long wall of building to the park. It is the second design produced as a result of this decision that gives the completed estate its rather casual relationship to Richmond Park.

Early municipal housing concerned itself with the housing of families, since it is they who find it most difficult to obtain the kind of dwelling they need at the price they can pay. This concern led to the attempt to find the ideal family dwelling and then repeat it over the entire site to be developed. Prewar estates, with rows of identical flats in identical blocks housing people of one age group, were the products of this search, and very dreary they were both to live in and to look at. Since the war, particularly in London, a reaction has taken place and the ideas of 'mixed development' has been evolved. This means that in each separate development a variety of dwellings is provided, which gives the tenant a possible choice and to a large extent houses a cross-section of age groups. The number of flats that are allowed to be built on a particular site is determined by the LCC planners and the percentage of different-sized flats is determined by the council's sociologists. So before the architects put pencil to paper the accommodation required is known. At Roehampton the breakdown was: flats with 1/2 bedrooms, 41 per cent; maisonettes with 2 bedrooms, 12 per cent; maisonettes with 3 bedrooms, 31 per cent; houses with 3/4 bedrooms, 14 per cent; old peoples' one-roomed houses, 2 per cent. In order to reap the economic advantages of repetition in construction, the architects decided not to mix different types of accommodation in one building. They therefore designed a different building type for each dwelling type.

The one-and-two bedroom flats that make up 41 per cent are in 15 towers. Such tall, thin housing towers are called point blocks by architects because, although they are large buildings, they cover only a small area on plan. Eight of the point blocks are in a cluster in the centre of the site and the remaining seven to the west. Each block is 12 storeys high and has four flats to each floor, two with two bedrooms each and two with only one. A central hallway on each floor provides access to the flats from the two lifts and there

A view across the great grassed open space showing the five maisonette blocks, which are staggered to give the occupants a better outlook.

154

The library, tucked underneath a slab block as seen from the access gallery to the flats over the shopping centre. Glass blocks, set in the domes of the library roof, ensure good inside lighting and provide a sparkle to the interior.

are two staircases to meet the fire regulations of the time. The ground floor is largely open in the Le Corbusier tradition, but is partly used as a store for prams and bicycles. The frame of the building is of concrete and on the ground floor and in the lift-machinery room on the roof the concrete is left in its natural state, straight from its wooden moulds, which are much more carefully made than those in a Le Corbusier building of similar date. The 11 identical floors of flats are made of precast concrete (made in moulds on the ground and lifted into position); these precast units are factory-made in steel moulds. The outer face on the completed building is the exposed top face of the concrete in the mould and this is carefully finished to a light colour by a mixture of Dorset shingle and Derbyshire spar using white cement and Reigate sand, These precast units are placed in the building in a way that reveals what is going on behind: one unit is bolted to the edge beam of the floor slabs and defines the ceiling and floor levels behind it; others are placed vertically between to show the height of the rooms and a long horizontal unit defines the balcony and acts as its balustrade.

The maisonettes with two bedrooms are grouped in five slab blocks which, architecturally, are clearly descended from Le Corbusier's building at Marseille. Two aspects of the Marseille building, however, did not seem to the architects to be appropriate to the English situation. At Marseille, living rooms face out on both sides of the block, whereas in England it is desirable to have them all on the sunny side. Also an interior access corridor like that at Marseille could easily degenerate into a noisy, smelly unpleasant space. At Roehampton the architects used a maisonette type that had recently been developed by the LCC, and variations of it had been used on other LCC estates. These maisonettes, as used in the Roehampton slab blocks, are admirably simple, but they have been little used in subsequent LCC estates because the external balcony access has not proved popular. Paradoxically it is the internal corridor access rejected by the Roehampton architects that is used on such post-Roehampton LCC schemes as Morris Walk, Woolwich.

Each maisonette at Roehampton is like a small house; there is an entrance hall (with a place for a pram), which is entered from the access gallery. Next to the hall there is a small working kitchen, and beyond is a dining/living room with a balcony extending the full width of the dwelling. And because the room above the living room is a bedroom with no balcony, the sun can come flooding in and the view out is of sky, not the underside of the balcony on the

The great chimney to the boilers, above, is placed at the north end of one of the maisonette blocks; the boiler house is set below road level.

The thin columns under the maisonette block, opposite, make them appear to sit lightly on the ground and the landscape passes under the buildings with the minimum of interruption. 157

The old people are housed in little one-room cottages, above, each with its own garden.

Left, one of the two clusters of point blocks. These towers are covered with thin concrete panels; horizontal panels show the floor positions and vertical panels define the room heights.

Opposite, the boiler house, a chunky concrete building with the lower side glazed to show off the boilers. These boilers provide central heating and hot water for the entire estate.

Left, two-storey terraces at Roehampton, each house with an open garden in front and private garden behind.

Right, the library, one of the one-off buildings. It is a massive concrete structure and tucks underneath a block of flats. Four-storey maisonette blocks can be seen beyond.

Below left, the education centre adjoining the single-storey cottages. All the dwellings at Roehampton are kept very simple since they are repeated many times; in contrast, the one-off buildings—the boiler house, the library and the community rooms—are highly modelled and individual.

floor above as in the point blocks of one-storey flats. On the upper level of the maisonette, there are bedrooms front and back, each running the full width of the dwelling and in the centre are an airing cupboard, W.C. and bathroom. These have no windows and are artificially lit and ventilated. The bedrooms on one side have access to a fire-escape. The construction is of concrete, and every other wall between the flats is ingeniously constructed in two separate skins, so that W.C.s, bathrooms and kitchens can back on to it and their waste, water and ventilation systems can run up and down the hollow space in the middle of the wall. Exterior concrete finishes are generally similar to the point blocks, with the addition of thin precast concrete members running vertically up the building and connecting the outer faces of the balconies. These are not structural, but define on the outside of the building the size of the individual dwellings within. Like the point blocks, the dimensions of these slab blocks are largely worked out according to Le Corbusier's *modulor*.

The buildings stand on sloping ground. This is taken up under the building by free-standing columns, which vary in length so that the ground can flow through at its own level. These columns are placed 12 feet apart under each wall separating the maisonettes above. Where this wall is solid, it is supported on two columns, but where the wall is hollow for the services, the three supporting columns within the hollow walls are taken down direct. Thus there are alternating rows of two and three columns, so that they appear staggered under the building. This arrangement is not only a logical expression of the structure above but is also important aesthetically, since the number of columns appears less than it is, so that the buildings seem to sit lightly on the ground. At the north end of one of the blocks is the boiler house, which provides heating and hot water to the whole estate. Here, after their restraint and economical common sense in the dwellings, the architects have let themselves go a bit: there is a flamboyant chimney-stack 100 feet high and the boilers themselves behind their glass wall under a tough, rugged concrete roof are a splendid sight, especially at night.

The three-bedroomed maisonettes are housed in four-storey blocks. These are built in a brick 'cross-wall construction'—the simplest possible form of construction with brick walls parallel to one another, spanned by floor and roof slabs. The ends of these brick cross-walls show on the elevations and this explains both the construction and the dimensions of the dwellings within. The

remainder of the elevation is made of glass so that it is obvious that it takes no load; the cross-wall construction is therefore made even clearer. Architecturally these buildings are not as rewarding as the others on the estate, but they are cheap to build because, with only four storeys, a lift is not needed. They are also popular with the tenants because half the dwellings have living rooms on the ground floor and private gardens.

The shopping centre with part of the library showing at the right.

162   The three- and four-bedroom houses are built in two-storey

terraces, generally similar in construction to the four-storey maisonettes. However the elevations are much less cluttered and they are altogether more successful architecturally. They have private walled gardens complete with brick garden sheds at the back. In an attempt to make the estate more mixed socially, 28 three-storey houses have also been built, giving more space and higher amenities for middle-class families.

The most attractive of the low buildings are the one-storey houses for old people. They are tiny dwellings consisting of a bed-sitting room with small kitchen, bathroom and fuel store. Construction is of brickwork painted white and the houses are linked together very informally so that they seem to cascade down the hill towards the old people's clubroom at the bottom. The informal siting is not entirely whimsical, for by staggering the little houses, it is possible to provide some privacy and form sunny sitting-out areas with little walls and flower beds. Yet because the houses themselves are modern and uncompromisingly part of the Roehampton scheme, there is no feeling of playing down to the occupants. In the clubroom, as in the boiler house, the architects have played with their concrete with less of the single-minded logic and economy than they applied to the housing; the resulting building is a delight.

Somehow Roehampton has joined together two elements: the influence of Le Corbusier, which is felt in the buildings, and the English landscape tradition, which was responsible for the site. This fusion of clean, modern buildings carefully but informally placed in a park setting gives the site its magical quality, whether it is seen from within the estate or viewed from Richmond Park.

When Roehampton was designed, it was assumed that few occupants of council dwellings would be able to afford cars, so little parking space was provided. Yet within ten years of completion there were so many cars that the whole elegant landscape is threatened. An architect's preliminary sketch of the shopping street shows one solitary Rolls-Royce on the road; if one visits it today, one will find a sea of Minis and Anglias parked bumper to bumper. In retrospect, it is obvious that the problem of the motor car has not been faced; it is equally clear that the four-storey blocks are tedious. Nonetheless it is as near as we have yet got, anywhere in the world, to a habitable, non-suburban, 20th-century environment. What other housing with equal charm, character and sense of space has been created since the Industrial Revolution? Rich or poor, the inhabitants of Alton West are a privileged class.

CHAPTER 11

FACTORY FOR THE CUMMINS ENGINE COMPANY

Yarm Road, Darlington, County Durham

Most great buildings of the past have not just grown old; they have grown old gracefully. Their materials have mellowed and time has given them a patina so that they become more beautiful with age. Modern buildings, built with machine-made products, have usually weathered badly; they resemble cars, whose bodywork is perfect when new and gradually deteriorates until it is scrapped. But buildings have to last longer than cars, for we are not yet rich enough to throw them away every few years, although we shall probably do so with some types of building in the future. Modern buildings are built and carefully finished; photographs are taken at the moment of completion, other architects come to see and write about them. Then the elements set to work and within a few years their appearance is spoilt; streaky concrete, flaking paintwork, corroded metal have taken all the precision out of the design. How enviously modern architects have looked back to the time when builders used Pentelic marble, travertine or Portland stone and long for industry to give them a material that would, like them, grow more beautiful with the years. Unfortunately, aluminium has pitted, plastic has gone brittle, stainless steel has not proved stainless, and owners are often faced with a crippling maintenance bill if they wish to keep their new buildings spick and span. So, incredible as it may seem when we consider the millions of pounds spent annually on building research, our buildings today are often less able to withstand the weather than the 'unscientific' buildings of a century or two ago.

The American architect Eero Saarinen once observed that pylons carrying power cables across Michigan were of unpainted steel that had been exposed to the elements for forty years without ill effect.

The John Deere building at Moline, Illinois, faced with a copper-steel alloy, which weathers dark brown making it one of the first modern buildings to grow old gracefully.

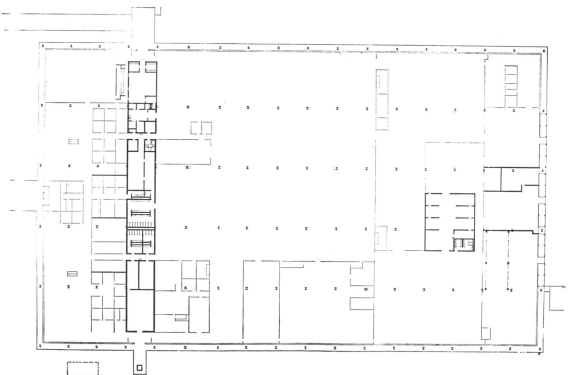

On enquiry he discovered that they were made out of Cor-ten, a type of steel alloy with a high copper content. When conventional mild steel rusts, the rust flakes off, exposing more steel and so on until all the steel has oxidised. Cor-ten starts to rust in the normal way, but the initial layer of oxidation forms a protective skin, which reduces further oxidation to a small and calculable amount. At the time Saarinen was designing in his office a new headquarters building for John Deere and Company, manufacturers of farm machinery, at Moline, in southern Illinois. He therefore determined to build 'an iron building for a farm-machinery manufacturer'—an evocative phrase calling up a picture of an old piece of farm machinery rusting in the corner of a field; it had to be rusting or the image

Opposite, top, a general view of the factory from Yarm Road. Note the fence around the site, set in a deep trench so that the buildings seem to stand in open fields.

Opposite, bottom, a plan showing how the brick service core divides the office space to the left from the factory space to the right. This arrangement enables the building to be extended sideways with office space, service core and factory area all growing in the same proportion.

Below, the entrance side with its columns set 60 feet apart and the main roof beams projecting beyond the columns.

would not ring true. Saarinen was a man who took risks, and used a material new to the building industry for a multi-million dollar building. In 1962 the John Deere building was finished, and today it stands rusting in its landscaped park—the first machine-made building to weather beautifully and acquire patina with age.

The John Deere building has sunshades of steel so that the material is everywhere dominant. For when designing this building Saarinen determined to create an architecture expressive of steel—just as at Marseille Le Corbusier had made an architecture expressive of concrete—and to a large measure he succeeded. It is always easy to be wise after the event, but in retrospect it seems fantastic that high-copper steel had been used since before the first World War for lorries, for railway trucks, for pylons, but not until after John Deere was it slowly adopted by the building industry as an alternative to ordinary mild steel, which must be painted year after year. Perhaps this is a manifestation of our specialised age when ideas do not cross easily from one field to another; or perhaps it is a result of the conservatism of the steelmen, who, trained to look on rust as an enemy, find it impossible to accept it as a friend.

Eero Saarinen always kept his eyes open for ideas that might be useful to the building industry; as architect to the Technical Center

Above, the main entrance approached by a broad walkway from the car park. Managers, visitors and factory workers all go into the same carpeted entrance and reception area.

Right, the roof deck is held clear above the main structure by short lengths of steel beam. These have the characteristic I-section profile to emphasise the steeliness of the building, and internally they provide a gap over the main roof beams so that air ducts and other services can be fixed under the roof.

for General Motors, he had an excellent opportunity to pirate the technical know-how and the design ideas of the carmakers and apply them to building. One of the many techniques he introduced to the building industry was 'gasket glazing'—the fixing of glass in extruded strips of Neoprene instead of window frames and putty. This is a quick, clean, neat operation and takes the building process one step nearer to the ideal of eliminating all messy trades from the site.

In 1961 Eero Saarinen died at the early age of 50. His office continued to complete the buildings under construction but Saarinen had stipulated that only buildings designed by him should be credited to him. His young associates Kevin Roche and John Dinkeloo therefore set up a new firm under their own names. Their first commission came from Irwin Miller, a knowledgeable and enthusiastic admirer of modern architecture and one of its most consistent patrons. Miller had first commissioned buildings from Eliel Saarinen, Eero's father. He then had a bank and a house built by the son, and when his company—Cummins Engine—needed a plant in England he retained his loyalty to the old firm. It was a great opportunity for Roche and Dinkeloo; it was also a great opportunity for Europe, for it brought the technological know-how of the Saarinen office across the Atlantic.

The town of Darlington had seen better days. It was a terminus for the world's first steam railway, but had had difficulty moving out of the steam age. And it had long since lost its technological leadership when Cummins Engine came to the town as a result of a government industrial development programme set up to encourage industry to settle in economically depressed areas. Since there was a high level of unemployment in the area, Cummins had no need to build a prestige building to attract staff, nor would a conspicious display of wealth have been appropriate. The completed building is a straightforward shed, but so simply planned and so elegantly put together that it is a minor masterpiece. There is a story that when in 1630 the Earl of Bedford was briefing his architect, Inigo Jones, for the design of St Paul's, Covent Garden, he said that he 'would not have it much better than a barn'; Jones replied that he would build 'the handsomest barn in England'. Similarly, the Cummins building is not much more than a shed, but it must be the handsomest shed in England.

The Cummins Engine Company assemble diesel engines in their Darlington building. For this, they needed a large factory space

Above, the broad roof overhang that keeps the high summer sun from overheating the building through the glass walls. Nothing will grow well under such an overhang so the building stands on a brick plinth as wide as the eaves.

170

Above, a close-up of a corner of the roof showing the way the steel rusts, forming patterns according to the degree of exposure in the same way as a building constructed of Portland stone weathers to a pattern made by the rain and wind that beat upon it.

Left, the boiler house chimney, faced with the same steel alloy as that used for the construction of the factory building.

with as few columns as possible so that production engineers could efficiently plan the work flow and replan it when the production lines changed. Cummins also required office space, both for their administrative staff and for their drawing office, as well as the usual factory amenities—canteen, car park and so on. These requirements are similar to those of hundreds of other companies, and might have resulted in yet another dreary industrial building. But Cummins's head is Irwin Miller, a man who is prepared to back his architects' ideas and to ensure that the company looked after its building once it was finished.

The site was a flat, rather uninteresting field east of Darlington on the road to Yarm. The atmosphere is so polluted by industrial waste that most building materials look squalid in a few years—not the most encouraging welcome for the young architects who had travelled three thousand miles from their office to the site.

The plan produced by the architects could not have been simpler. They recognised that most people would arrive by car; so the

Opposite, the carpeted reception area. There is very little internal partitioning, and that which does exist is low and is constructed in the same way as the glass skin of the building.

The office area (below) and the factory area (shown overleaf) have the same structure and lighting and are both large open areas with the same orderly arrangement of tables and benches.

entrance to the site leads directly into the car park while the main entrance to the building is at the side of the car park. This entrance leads directly into the office area, a large open, carpeted space with no private offices, but glazed screens to define areas used for conferences or interviewing. This open space has all the 'togetherness' of a smooth American office, but there is plenty of English untidiness and broad North Country voices to dispel any illusions that this is Massachusetts. Behind the office area is a mechanical core, an area containing lavatories, heating plant and so on; beyond this is the factory itself, covering an area of 158,000 square feet. The building is placed off-centre on its site, nearer to the road, so that it can expand on the other side. As can be seen by looking at the plan (p. 166), by expanding sideways, factory, mechanical core, offices and car park can all grow together in the same proportion.

The architects have built their shed of steel, the most economical— 174 and elegant—material for a long-span, single-storey structure.

In the factory area, as in the office area, only the problem of noise causes departures from the open-space idea. Small glass rooms are placed in the office area for conference and interviews, while in the factory comparable rooms contain noisy or messy operations.

Remembering the corrosive atmosphere in Darlington and the disruption of work caused by repainting, they decided to use an oxidising steel similar to the Cor-ten used by the Saarinen office in the John Deere building at Moline. This was more expensive than mild steel, but the cost could be offset by lower maintenance bills. The architects then went all out to make the 'steeliness' of the building as apparent as possible. Since steel sections are traditionally in the form of I-shaped beams, members of this shape are used everywhere; the main roof beams, for example, project outside the building, partly in readiness to receive a similar beam that would be welded on when the building was extended, but principally to emphasise the steely character.

The main supporting columns are 60 feet apart in one direction and 30 feet apart in the other; the resulting bay area allows great freedom of arrangement for both offices and factory. By using the same structure for both factory and office space, the building is made even more flexible, since the amount of space devoted to one or the other may be varied. Deep steel I-beams span between the tops of the columns to support the roof, whose structure is made up of smaller I-beams. These do not rest directly on the deep beams, which might look dull and would not allow space for the ventilating ducts to pass over the main beam; each roof beam is therefore supported on a short length of 18-inch-deep I-beam left completely exposed. This simple device greatly increases the 'steeliness' of the building as well as fulfilling a functional purpose. The main structure and the roof are both extended several feet beyond the building to allow for future expansion; to keep out the heat of the sun when it is high in summer; and to reduce the glare from the sky. Because during the first year of exposure some rust may be washed off the steel and stain the ground, the whole building has been surrounded by a broad step of dark coloured bricks which do not absorb the stain and in addition are useful as a base for the window cleaner.

The outside skin of the building is glass in framing members of oxidising steel; the top and bottom members are I-beams while the verticals, 6 feet apart, are T-shaped sections. These windows are too large to be glazed economically with a single sheet of glass, so the area between each pair of uprights has been divided horizontally into seven; the quarter of an inch thick plate glass is fixed in place with black Neoprene gaskets like the windows of a car, but on a very much larger scale. These gaskets are welded up complete for each 20 foot by 6 foot window. The horizontals have no metal in them;

they merely join the horizontal glass sections and keep them water-proof. The strength of the glass itself is used to span the 6 feet from steel upright to steel upright. If anyone leans against the glass it bends alarmingly; in short, the whole glazing system has been pushed by the architects to the absolute limit. None of the windows open since the building is mechanically ventilated. Indeed Neoprene grips the glass so tightly that—perhaps for the first time in England—the ancient dream of a glass wall without draughts has been realised.

In the office space a few areas are divided by screens constructed in exactly the same way as the outer skin of the building. The screens are kept down to a height of 8 feet, so that the main structure is not disturbed by the partitioning inside.

Around the bottom of the glass outer skin runs a hot pipe to offset heat lost through the glass. But most of the heat and all the ventilation is from units mounted on the roof, each unit serving six of the 60 foot by 30 foot bays. This local system of heating was chosen in preference to a centralised system because it can be added to more easily if the building is extended.

The American landscape office of Dan Kiley was responsible for the landscaping of the site. Hundreds of trees have been planted, which have not yet grown to full maturity. These trees are some distance from the building, and are used to conceal the car park and to separate the site from the road. It was considered necessary to surround the site with a high wire fence for security; this could easily have given the site a prison-like appearance, but the landscape architects have cunningly concealed the fence at the bottom of a deep artificial ditch. Thus the factory appears to be set in a lawn. which spreads as far as the road and the surrounding countryside without a barrier.

By the time the building was finished in 1966, the steel had already lost its silver colour and acquired its layer of protective rust—a beautiful warm dark brown colour, which neither rain nor sun nor polluted air will harm. The square chimney, also cased in the same steel, presents a wonderful gradation of colour from the very exposed top to the more protected bottom. And the clean, pristine look will remain, because not only is this a building that will age beautifully but also the management will not let it deteriorate into the usual industrial squalor, with corrugated iron lean-tos and cars parked on the grass. The building will also contribute to its own preservation by being flexible enough to cope with most changes in function or production methods in the years to come.

A corner view of the Cummins Engine Factory at Darlington showing the glass skin of the building set well back under the rusty steel frame that carries the roof.

CHAPTER 12

EIGHT COURTHOUSES IN CHICAGO

1366–1380, East Madison Park, Chicago, Ill.

The courthouse is a reversal of the typical suburban house, where the garden covers the site and the house stands in the garden; in a courthouse, however, it is the house that covers the site and the garden that is inside the house.

Some ideas in building become outmoded in a few years; others appear to have a timeless validity. Such building types as the castle and the palace have come and gone, but the concept of a home with blank walls on to the city streets outside but opening on to a central garden inside would seem to satisfy a perennial need—that of the weary man seeking peace in a private garden in his own home in the heart of a city. The idea has reappeared in different places at different times. Excavations at Pompeii have uncovered many beautiful *atrium* houses. (*Atrium* is the Latin word for such a courtyard garden.) In Kyoto, ancient capital of Japan, there still remain whole districts of fine old houses planned around elegantly planted but small gardens. Again, in the Arab countries of the Middle East, there is a tradition of living in houses with central courtyards.

The courthouse idea was revived in the 1930s by Mies van der Rohe in a series of beautiful designs for individual houses and groups of houses. Earlier houses designed by Mies had internal walls extending out into the garden like the sails of a windmill. Such walls, however, would have cut the garden into separate areas, and in the small lots on which most houses stand the effect needed is of more space, not less. In his courthouses Mies reversed the procedure by putting a brick wall completely around the site, giving privacy within. Inside this enclosure, the house is supported partly on the brick wall and partly on internal steel columns while the wall between house and garden was made entirely from glass, so that, from inside, the rooms

Right, a high-level view of the Chicago courthouses looking across the central service area. Courtyards to two of the houses beyond can just be seen.

Another photograph taken from above, below right, explains the development: two blocks of four dwellings, each one storey high and without any windows in its outside walls. Inside each block can be seen the little patio gardens.

would appear spacious since their limits would seem to extend to the courtyard walls. The first courthouse scheme put forward by Mies was a row designed in 1931, in which each square plot is surrounded by a brick wall; inside an L-shaped house extends along two sides of the square and the rooms look on to a square court. Such an arrangement may provide privacy from the outside world, but the occupants of one side of the court overlook those on the other and so have little privacy from one another. Mies tackled this situation in his next scheme, and in 1934 he designed a house with three courts. As in the 1931 design, the house itself is the roofed section of a totally walled site, but the house is shaped like a T to form three courtyards so there is little overlooking. In 1935 Mies was asked to build such a courthouse for the Hubbe family in Magdeburg. The designs were prepared, but because the Hitler government was in favour of a more 'nationalist' type of architecture at the time, neither the Hubbe house nor any of the other courthouses was built.

Good ideas travel fast in the architectural world, however, and often projects have as much influence as completed buildings. As a result of Mies's work, houses designed round courts became one of the stock answers to housing problems produced by students in schools of architecture. Yet when architects tried to build them, they were discouraged by building regulations, with antiquated rules about space around and between houses, which exist in most technologically advanced societies. In 1950 the architect Philip Johnson built an exotic guest house with an elegant court for John D. Rockefeller III in midtown Manhattan. But by building a single-storey house surrounded by skyscrapers on some of the world's most expensive land, the courthouse was made to seem a plaything for millionaires. Mies meanwhile had been teaching in Chicago since 1938; it was inevitable, therefore, that sooner or later, one of his students would actually build the courthouses he had learnt to design as a student.

In the 1950s, a group in Chicago consisting of high-school teachers, architects and their friends amalgamated with the purpose of building houses for themselves. One of the group was the architect Y. C. Wong, a former pupil of Mies van der Rohe and a believer in the courthouse as a solution to urban living. The group called itself Atrium Homes Inc. and acquired a site on Chicago's South Side in an area called Hyde Park, which had declined from being a respectable residential district and was being redeveloped. But

From a side street, above, the houses look like garden walls.

Opposite, a view looking across the courtyard from one part of the house to another. 181

although the site was within the Hyde Park–Kenwood renewal district, Atrium Homes Inc. was not granted a redevelopment subsidy because the Federal Housing Authority was suspicious of the design; the householders also had trouble obtaining mortgages. Apparently the local loan associations regarded the atrium house, one of the oldest ways of home building in the world, as too modern for Chicago! Eventually, however, a sympathetic loan association was found; even so, each of the eight householders had to put down $10,000 towards the $32,500 cost of his house and plot.

No architect has yet designed the perfect house and probably no such thing exists—we all differ too much in our tastes, our needs and our moods for standard solutions to work. Wong has not tried to tell his friends how they should live, but each of the eight occupants has accepted the brick perimeter wall and the courtyard as immutable and planned his individual rooms inside it. Each house therefore has an austere exterior identical to its neighbour, but inside it is tailor-made for its owner and as personal as he wishes. This scheme resolves one of the principal problems of housing: people want their houses to be individual and personal, but a street of houses each trying to look 'different' is a chaotic and usually ugly street. Wong's street façades are extremely calm and disciplined, though inside people can arrange their houses as they please without destroying the orderly quality of their environment.

Yet even allowing for individual preferences, it will be seen from the plan that each of the eight occupants has chosen to have his

Below left, the entrance. The dark, deeply recessed, unglazed entrance doors set in the windowless walls emphasise that these are private places, very different from the typical American surburban home.

Below, the service area, centrally placed among the eight houses with the eight 'back doors'. This is for tradesmen and is used as a play space for children, but the privacy of the dwellings is maintained in exactly the same way as it is on the side streets of the block.

living room along the side of the court with bedrooms across the ends. We find too that in every plan the two corners are without windows and are therefore occupied by the kitchen and a bathroom, lit by roof lights. A bathroom without an outlook is a very reasonable proposition, but since kitchens in family houses are occupied for four or five hours a day, one may question whether the architect has not been too severe on his clients. The pursuit of perfection in architectural form has gone astray if it confines people to dark corners. However, the other rooms in the house are so calm and pleasant that one forgives the kitchen. All these rooms look out on to the court. As the architect points out, the atrium 'belongs' to every room in the house. Thus the use of the garden space is tripled, and because every room seems to extend to the far side of the atrium, rooms of modest size appear spacious. This flow of space is enhanced by making floors the same level inside and outside; by glazing from

By standing on the roof the photographer has invaded the privacy of the houses and can peer down into one of the courtyard gardens. Walls between house and garden are all glass to compensate for the solid walls to the outside.

183

floor to ceiling with large panes of glass; and by careful attention to the lights in the atrium. At night, when the atrium lights are turned on and the inside lights are off, the glass seems to disappear entirely. The occupants can then eat their meals in air-conditioned comfort and enjoy the weather a few feet away without any of the visual barriers of ordinary buildings. This wonderful arrangement is achieved at the sacrifice of privacy, since all the rooms of a house are glazed on to the same atrium. But the kind of family who would choose to live in such a house, having barricaded themselves in against the world outside, are less likely to be seeking privacy from one another; and if they are, they can always pull the curtains.

As the corollary to the glass walls on to the atrium, the walls surrounding each dwelling are entirely solid; it is the combination of these two types of wall that makes the introverted house. The brick exterior wall of each house is pierced twice, once by an un-glazed door leading into a central courtyard shared by all eight houses. This courtyard, which is itself walled off from the street and entered through a door at each end, serves as a common garden, an entrance for tradesmen and a traffic-free playground for children. The entrance doors are deliberately made very austere to contrast with the luxury and openness inside. One resident has described how visitors often approach with 'doubt, uncertainty, sometimes

Snow adds delight to the outlook on to the court, shown above, and the owner, with his central heating, can contemplate his tiny landscape and control its lighting.

Above left, a general interior view looking across the living room into the garden court and through to the bedroom beyond. The picture emphasises the privacy afforded by the layout, for the houses stand on a main road in a dense area of Chicago.

even hostility showing in their faces. It is a pleasure to see the sudden change of expression . . . as they see the atrium and the idea comes through.'

The structure of each house is steel and brick. It is also, as one would expect from a pupil of Mies van der Rohe, very clear and, visually, an important part of the design. Brick is used for the perimeter wall of each individual house; the mass of brickwork provides excellent sound insulation between dwellings and would prevent a fire spreading from house to house while its apparent solidarity creates a rather fortress-like appearance from the street— an appropriate impression for such an introverted building. Inside its solid enclosing brick wall, each house is framed in steel. The construction is therefore light and open, so that walls may be placed in different positions in different houses without affecting the standardised construction and, above all, so that the walls on to the atrium can be entirely glazed.

Mies van der Rohe taught his students to aim for perfection in

A view from an entrance hall into the living room and garden court. Some of the houses are beautifully furnished; this one has chairs designed by Mies van der Rohe and a Le Corbusier tapestry.

building construction. They had to spend long hours producing immaculate drawings of sections of buildings where all parts are exquisitely joined together. As a result, there has now grown up in Chicago a generation of architects whose skill in the art of building is considerable. This skill is coupled with an architecture of extreme reticence. Generally speaking, the simpler the form of the building the more important it is that the little there is should be well put together. Architect Wong measured up well to these standards, for everywhere in the courthouses we see building of very high quality. Such careful thought is well repaid, for in such a simple building, one piece of shoddy construction, one area of unpleasant proportion, one slip in the choice of colours, and all is lost. A more complex architecture, that of Le Corbusier for example, can absorb faults; the pristine architecture of the new Chicago school cannot. Not only are the courthouses well built (Wong has in fact shown his master a thing or two, for they are much better constructed than many of Mies van der Rohe's own buildings), but the materials are treated with severe restraint. The exterior wall is of light tan bricks, with every sixth course laid as headers (that is, with its head turned towards the face of the wall). This wall is capped by a band of stone, which measures the thickness of the roof structure; this is topped with a copper edging as a trim to the waterproof roof membrane. Inside, the steelwork is exposed and painted and the glazing is set in frames of aluminium.

Americans expect a high standard of mechanical services in their buildings. The houses are fully air-conditioned, so that the temperature can be cool on hot humid Chicago summer days while in winter, warm air comes out of grilles in the floor below the windows to provide heat and to prevent condensation. Because of the mechanical ventilation system, the courtyard windows are not required to let in fresh air; they are very simple and consist merely of a few large sheets of glass, which can slide open to provide access to the court or natural ventilation when preferred. Artificial lighting is of a high standard. (As we have seen, the bathrooms and utility rooms rely entirely on artificial lighting.) Relieved of the necessity of providing light and air, the court is a delightful place, which the owner can plant or pave or make into a pool as he prefers—an area to sit in or to look at, with fountains splashing in summer, thick snow in winter, and brightly floodlit in the evening. In a city of five million people, the lucky owner has achieved the peace of a monastery.

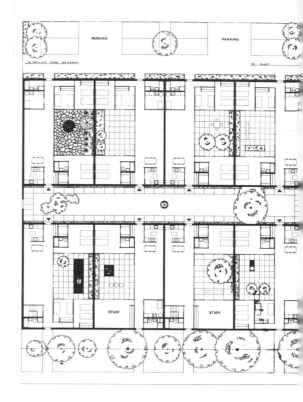

A plan of the houses showing that although the fortress-like outside walls and the garden courts are identical for all eight houses, the internal arrangements are different in accordance with the needs and preferences of the individual owners.

Further reading list

Banham, Reyner, *Guide to Modern Architecture*; London, 1962
Blake, Peter, *Mies van der Rohe: The Architecture of Structure;
    Le Corbusier; Frank Lloyd Wright: Architecture and Space*; Harmondsworth, 1963
Cantacazino, Sherban, *Great Modern Architecture*; New York, 1966
Jacobus, John, *Twentieth Century Architecture*; London, 1966
McCallum, Ian, *Architecture U.S.A.*; London, 1959
Richards, J. M., *Introduction to Modern Architecture*; London, 1940

Glossary

Bauhaus: the school of architecture and industrial design that flourished in Germany during the 1920s.

cantilever: a horizontal structural member projecting beyond its support.

cladding: the external, non-structural skin of a framed building.

column: a vertical support. A more sophisticated word for 'post'.

court, courtyard: an unroofed space in the centre of a building.

curtain wall: the lightweight skin of a framed building, usually suspended floor by floor, hence the name.

flexibility: the ability of a building to be easily changed to accommodate new requirements.

formwork: the mould into which concrete is poured. When the concrete is set the formwork is removed.

frame: the skeleton of a building (usually steel or reinforced concrete), which carries its load on beams and columns, as opposed to a load-bearing masonry building, which carries the load on walls and has no frame.

grid: a regular arrangement of imaginary lines on which the different parts of a building are made to fit.

mullion: a vertical division between windows.

plant: mechanical equipment.

precast concrete: concrete that is poured and has set before being placed in the building, as opposed to 'in situ' or 'poured in place' concrete, which is poured and left to set in its final position.

reinforced concrete: concrete reinforced with steel rods.

services: plumbing, electricity, gas pipes, lift machinery and so on.

siding: an American term for wood or metal cladding.

structure: the part of a building that carries the load to the ground.

187

Index

Figures in italics refer to illustrations

Acknowledgements

Key to picture positions: (*T*) top, (*B*) bottom, (*L*) left, (*R*) right. Numbers refer to the pages on which the pictures appear.

Alpha Photo Associates 53; Architectural Press 17(*B*), 20, 26(*T*), 26(*B*), 34, 99(*T*), 100, 101, 102, 103, 104, 105, 106, 107, 108; Morley Baer 10; Edward L. Barnes 30(*B*); Bauhaus Archiv 15; Leonardo Bezzola 137, 146, 149; Werner Blaser 50, 51, 54, 61–62; Brecht-Einzig Ltd. 33; Camera Press 159(*B*); Cement and Concrete Association 77(*B*), 78(*T*), 79(*B*); Domus 82(*BL*); Charles Eames 112(*T*), 112(*B*), 113, 114(*T*), 114(*B*), 117(*T*), 117(*B*), 118(*T*), 118(*B*), 119, 120, 121, 122; John Ebstel 14; Alexandre Georges 13(*B*), 55, 58; G.L.C. Photographic Library 151, 155(*T*), 155(*B*), 157, 158, 159(*T*), 160(*B*), 161; Hamlyn Archive 79(*T*); Hedrich-Blessing 19, 23(*B*), 27, 35(*BL*), 66, 69(*T*), 69(*B*), 70(*T*), 71, 72(*T*), 72(*R*), 74(*T*), 74(*C*), 75(*T*), 75(*B*), 179(*T*), 181, 182(*L*), 182(*R*), 183, 184(*L*); Lucien Hervé 17(*T*), 24, 39(*T*), 40, 41(*TL*), 41(*TR*), 42, 43, 44, 45, 46, 49; M. Holford 96, 152, 156, 160(*T*), 162, 177; Illinois Institute of Technology 65, 73, 74(*B*); Arne Jacobsen 31(*L*); Dale D. Klaus 87, 93; Balthazar Korab 166, 167, 168, 169, 170, 171(*L*), 171(*T*), 172, 173; Leco Photo Service 31(*R*), 86(*T*), 86(*R*), 88(*TR*), 88(*TL*), 88(*B*), 90; R. Moncalvo 80; Christian Moser 141; Museum of Modern Art 8, 47; P. Nervi 76(*T*), 76(*B*), 81, 82(*R*), 83; Rondal Partridge 35(*BL*); Philipson Studios 174; Oscar Savio 77(*T*); Julius Shulman 25, 29, 57; Julius Shulman, courtesy of Richard J. Neutra 16, 21; Arthur Siegel 179(*B*), 184(*R*), 185; Skidmore, Owings and Merrill 12, 30(*T*); Ezra Stoller 11, 13(*T*), 23(*T*), 28, 35, 56, 59(*T*), 59(*B*), 63, 127(*T*), 127(*B*), 128(*T*), 128(*B*), 129, 130, 131, 135, 165; Union Tank Car Company 91, 92, 94, 95; Upjohn Company 124, 126, 132; Vasari 82(*TL*); John Webb 99(*B*); A. Winkler 138(*T*), 138(*B*), 140, 142, 143, 144, 145, 147(*B*); John Winter 32, 78(*B*), 110, 147(*T*).